The Westcountryr

A REGISTER AND RECORD OF THE WE⸍⸍⸍⸍⸍⸍
TRADING KETCHES AND SEVERN TROWS
1780 – 1986

© Gordon Mote

Dedicated to the memory of Reg Williams, Mate
of the ketch *Enid*, with whom I first went to sea.

CONTENTS

Front cover: "The *Dido C* passing old
Braunton Lighthouse". Watercolour by
North Devon artist William Atkins who
sailed in this vessel with his grandfather,
when a boy. (Copyright – the artist).

First published in 1986 by Badger Books, Bideford, North Devon
Typeset by Lens Typesetting, Bideford, North Devon
Printed by Maslands Printers, Tiverton

FOREWORD

by

DR BASIL GREENHILL, C.B., C.M.G., F.S.A., F.R.Hist.S.

Joint Chairman Exeter University Maritime History Project.
Formerly Director the National Maritime Museum

I am glad that Gordon Mote has found time from a busy professional life to compile this useful register of West of England trading ketches and trows. These vessels were such a feature of one's youth on the shores of the Bristol Channel that it is not difficult to share Gordon Mote's enthusiasm for them. I knew nearly all the ketches and trows which survived into the 1930's and was lucky enough to make passages in one or two of them. They were still a great feature of the Channel in those days, their grey sails and black hulls showing against the greens of the Devon and Somerset shores and the regular thump of their semi-diesel engines could be heard on almost every tide as they went up to Bristol, Lydney, Sharpness, or even occasionally still into little places like Lympsham Quay, where I saw the *Democrat* discharging Lydney coal as late as 1942.

The reader may well wonder why small wooden sailing vessels survived in trade right into the middle of this century. Their owners, masters and men (often the same people) sailing "by the thirds" were partners in a joint venture. Under this system the owner took one third of the gross freight and (to put it simply) maintained the vessel while the master took the other two thirds and ran her with it. In this way they ground the last dividends out of an investment made many years before by sheer hard work. The vessels were most of them old, some like the *Maude* and the *Two Sisters* very old, and some in such a state they were hard to keep at sea. But a maritime community such as Braunton and Appledore were willing to hang on to its tonnage until it was clear that more money could be made by selling them and investing ashore – and the sale value of the older vessels was very small, if, indeed, they could be sold at all.

A second factor in their survival was P.K. Harris's yard at Appledore, then run by three brothers, Fred, Percy and Sidney, who were good friends of mine. They had the reputation all around the coast of doing a good cheap job on a vessel to keep her working at sea and the survival of the ketches until the Second World War was to no small extent the result of their work. Because of the yard and the ketches and schooners Appledore kept its character as a community largely dependant on wooden sailing vessels right down to the 1940's.

Gordon Mote's book tells some of this story and is a useful contribution to the maritime history of the south-west.

St Dominic, Cornwall 1986   **BASIL GREENHILL**

About the Author

Gordon Mote, LDS, RCS Eng., has had a lifelong association with the sea. Much of his youth was spent in North Devon, where he was given his first taste of sailing in the Braunton-owned ketch *Enid.* Since then, despite a career as a dental surgeon, he has spent as much time as possible at sea, sailing either his own or other people's yachts. Now retired and living in East Anglia, Gordon Mote spends his summers sailing and his winters travelling the world on deep sea freighters. He is a well known navigator in both coastal and deep sea waters – and when forced to stay ashore, he wiles away the time making ship's models – and researching this book on ketches.

Author and Reg Williams at the wheel of the Enid

Acknowledgements

My thanks go to various institutions which were the source of details of many vessels:

The National Maritime Museum,
Lloyds Register of Shipping,
Exeter City Library,
North Devon Maritime Museum,
Padstow Museum,
Bude Museum,
Watchet Museum,
Ilfracombe Museum,
Folk Museum Gloucester,
Athenaeum at Barnstaple and
   Braunton Museum, North Devon.

I am particularly indebted to Lieut Commander John Gammon M.B.E., R.N. (RTD) Curator of Braunton Museum for much information and for providing me with some of the illustrations used in the book. My gratitude also to Stanley Rogers for extracts from his Notes on Braunton's Seagoing Trade, the North Devon Museum Trust for permission to reproduce 'The Torridge Hulks' chart, to Dr Basil Greenhill for much helpful advice and encouragement, to Mrs Liz Temple Cox for the typing, to Monmouth District Council Museums service for permission to reproduce the extract from the information sheet 'Trows of Severn and Wye' produced by Chepstow Museum and to Capt Peter Herbert for many photographs.

Sources

Mercantile Navy List and Maritime Directories 1857-1940.
Lloyds Register 1800-1920.
Port Transcipts at National Maritime Museum.
   Graham Farr & Others.
Lloyds Weekly Casualty Reports.
'Shipbuilding In North Devon.'
National Maritime Museum.
'The Bude Canal.'
   Helen Harris & Monica Ellis.
'Devon Shipwrecks.'
   Richard Lard.
'Braunton Ships And Seamen.'
   S E Ellacott.
'West Country Coasting Ketches.'
   W J Slade & Basil Greenhill.
'Out Of Appledore.'
   W J Slade.
'The Last Of The Sailing Coasters.'
   Edmund Eglington.
'No Gallant Ship.'
   M R Bouquet.
'West Country Sail.'
   M R Bouquet.
'Ships and Harbours of Exmoor.'
   Grahame Farr.
'Gloucester Docks.'
   H Conway Jones.
'The Story Of Bude Haven.'
   Rennie Bere.
'Goodnight Irene.'
   Dr L Morrish.

Ilfracombe Harbour 1880

OF ALL THE VARIOUS WOODEN MERCHANT SHIPS

that evolved over the centuries, the Westcountry Ketches and Severn Trows alone were specifically developed for the trades of the Westcountry, the Bristol Channel and Severn Estuary. Few other rigs, such as the sloops and smacks from which they evolved, competed with them, trading as they did to the small ports and beaches of the area.

They were built cheaply and carried a wide variety of cargoes at a time before a good road system had been developed for the movement of bulk cargoes. The men who manned them lived a hard life with no dole money when unemployed and no pensions to look forward to. There was no limit to their working hours and they had to be able to do the majority of the maintenance on their ships themselves with skills passed down from father to son.

Few exceeded 100 net registered tons and in

4

most cases they were small vessels of under 50 net registered tons. Ownership was often a family affair or a consortium of local men who formed a group of shareholders.

The ketch rig with its two masts, the mainmast and the mizzen, was a simple and easily handled rig, and the foremast was usually in two parts, the lower mast and a topmast which overlapped it. This overlap being known as the doubling. In later days rigs were cut down as engines were installed and the mainmast was replaced with a single mast. They became known as pole masted. The mizzen was invariably a pole mast though on occasions a fidded mizzen topmast was sometimes fitted. The mainsail and mizzen sails were set on gaffs and booms and above the mainsail a gaff topsail, usually square-headed, but sometimes jib-headed, was set. They normally carried four headsails, sometimes only three, and they were known as the staysail, the standing jib, the boom jib and the flying jib.

An advantage of the ketch rig over such as the schooners, the brigs and brigantines was that they could be managed with a smaller crew, freight rates were so low this was an important factor in keeping operating costs down, and whilst not so certain in stays (tacking through the wind) than those ships that carried square sails. Many ships built as schooners were subsequently converted to ketch rig.

The ships developed into two groups, one was known as the Down-Homers who traded basically in the Bristol Channel and slightly further afield in the summer, and the other group, the larger ketches, traded around the coasts of the United Kingdom and to the Continent. The Down-Homers descended from the brigs and brigantines of earlier days. Many of the ships as they grew older required continual pumping especially when the hull worked in a seaway and it was not uncommon to put the ship on the mud to fill the seams and reduce the amount of water she was making. Despite this, as will be seen many traded to a ripe old age.

The usual complement was made up of the Master who might also be owner or part owner, a mate and a boy, and in many cases they were manned by a family, the master's wife living on board. Insurance in the main was effected in an economical fashion through the operation of mutual local co-operative clubs. One of the best known was the Braunton Shipowners Mutual Insurance Association. This was for many years the home port of very many of the ships.

Along the North Somerset, North Devon and Cornish Coast can still be seen the remains of the old lime kilns which needed both coal and limestone for their operation, to supply lime for the farmers and for housebuilding, and the materials were brought by the ketches which ran to the open beaches and coves of these coasts. This was a dangerous trade and because of the risks from bad weather was mostly confined to the summer months. In the case of cargoes discharged outside the summer months the insurance clubs would often reduce their liabilities or would even not pay out at all.

Living conditions, particularly in the smaller ships, were rough and particularly hard in the winter. In the small space of the foc'sle lived very often three men; cooking was done on a small coal stove and as there was no laid down scale of food for seamen in those days, it was often of the cheapest variety supplemented by what they could scrounge and by their own efforts at fishing. Sanitary arrangements were virtually non-existent being confined to a bucket in the foc'sle.

Ocean Gem at Rolle Quay, Barnstaple

One of the most important cargoes carried by the ships was to supply the Westcountry with coal, and much of this was brought from Lydney in Gloucestershire. The coal was cheap there and came from the Forest of Dean.

These vessels were built as economically as possible in small yards and building sites on the river banks of the ports all along the coasts by local labour and mostly with local materials, and required the skills of those who owned and sailed them to maintain them in working condition. They could easily be damaged if cargo was not properly stowed and the ship carefully berthed when in harbour.

Whilst for economic reasons their numbers had severely declined by the outbreak of World War II, handling by crews not accustomed to the vessels when most were requisitioned for defence purposes by the Services, spelt the death knell for most of those still in trade and by the end of the war few were left fit to continue trading.

My association with the Westcountry ketches commenced in the 1930's when as a boy I spent many holidays at Georgeham, North Devon. I saw and photographed many of them at Barnstaple, Braunton, Bideford and Appledore and was fortunate to know

Roland Chichester, then part owner with his mother, and previously by his father, of the ketch *Enid* trading between Barnstaple and other North Devon ports, to South Wales carrying cargoes of sand, coal and basic slag. My first seagoing experience was on the *Enid* and I sailed on her before and after the 1939–45 War.

The history of the ketches has been most thoroughly researched and recorded in a number of books, most notably by W.J. Slade and Basil Greenhill in their 'Out of Appledore' and 'West Country Coasting Ketches', Michael Bouquet in his 'No Gallant Ship' and 'West Country Sail', Edmund Eglington in his 'Last of The Sailing Coasters' and S.E. Ellacott in his 'Braunton Story 3'. To all of them I make acknowledgement for material used in this book.

There has not, however, been compiled a complete register recording the vessels built during the 18th, 19th and 20th centuries and this book is an attempt to do so.

Whilst research from the Mercantile Navy Lists and Maritime Directories and Lloyds Registers has revealed over 500 ships and this register with some details of their histories with photographs is as complete as possible, there could be others not traced. It includes Bristol Channel Trows. I have endeavoured to ensure accuracy in compiling these details but difficulty in tracing some of the earliest ships makes it possible that some errors may have crept in.

It is my hope that this book may be a worthwhile addition to the literature of these coasting sailing ships which traded in the West Country during nearly two hundred years.

The last one to carry cargo was, I believe, the *Emily Barratt* which was also the last wooden merchant ketch built in the United

Emily Barratt, Bude 1960

Kingdom, and in 1983 was brought to Maldon, Essex, for restoration as a sail training ship.

The others still afloat in 1985 are, the *Garlandstone* restored at Porthmadoc, the *Irene* and the *Bessie Ellen* in Danish waters. These ships were the last ones which, over the centuries, traded under sail to the beaches, harbours and quays of the Westcountry. In their younger days some traded across the Atlantic to Newfoundland and to the Continent and Irish ports. Many carried a square sail set on a temporary yard for running before a following wind. They were manned by two men and a boy or sometimes only a master and mate. Roller reefing was introduced about the beginning of the century and large gaff topsails were usually carried. As engines became more common during and after the Great War rigs were reduced by dispensing with topmasts and the introduction of Bermudan rig on mizzen masts. The *Enid* was also Bermudan rigged on the main mast. The number of headsails was similarly reduced. Many of the ships

Lewisman

In 1912 approximately 150 ketches were in commission. None were lost by enemy action during the Second World War 1939-45, and the following were still in commission in 1947.

Agnes	*Halcyon*
Bessie Ellen	*Hanna*
C.F.H.	*Irene*
Clara May	*Lewisman*
Crown of Denmark	*Mary Eliezer*
Democrat	*Mary Stewart*
Emily Barratt	*Maude*
Emma Louise	*Roselyne*
Enid	*St Austell*
Florette	*Traly*
Garlandstone	

were owned at Braunton, North Devon and up to the second world war up to a dozen were regularly to be seen lying between cargoes in the Pill, the creek leading from the River Taw to Braunton. A list of ships registered there is in appendix II.

During the second world war a number served as supply ships to the R.N. and others as balloon barrage ships. The following extract is taken from 'Roof Over Britain'.

"Life in a waterborne barrage varies with the geographic situation. In a typical estuary balloons fly from barges, drifters and ketches. Vessels mobile and ready to move day or night. Civilian crews for the vessel and a crew of 3 or 4 airmen with a corporal in charge. The winch generally contained in the hold. Ten to fourteen days at sea at a time and fitted with radios. The manufacture of models, carpentry and metalwork occupy their spare time."

Some of the ketches were first rigged as sloops, smacks, brigantines, polacca schooners, fore and aft schooners and dandys but during the latter part of the nineteenth century the ketch rig became the rig most commonly adopted. Built for long service, some such as the Severn Trow *Jane* built 1800 and not broken up until 1939, and the *Ceres* built 1811 and lost 1936, lasted well into their second century.

During the days of poor roads and transport these little ships carried by sea a large part of the goods to and from the Westcountry, coal and bricks from South Wales and Somerset to Cornwall and Devon, wheat and bagged flour from Avonmouth, bricks and tiles to Liverpool and Ireland, sand to South Wales for building and china clay from South Devon. Now, however, the juggernaut and the lorry have emptied the seas and ports of these little ships and they are history.

The following is an account of a voyage I made on the *Enid* of Barnstaple in 1939, and demonstrates life on board a typical ketch in those days. I joined the ship at Braunton Pill on Saturday, 29th July, 1939, where she was lying with a cargo of slag for discharge at Rolle Quay, Barnstaple. The skipper and part owner with his mother was Roland Chichester of Georgeham, N. Devon, who had, at 35 years of age, been at sea in the coasting trade for some 20 years. His father had previously owned the *Enid* trading under sail for many years before installing a 30 b.h.p. hot bulb diesel engine. The mate was Reg Williams of Wrafton, 45 years old, who had been in sailing coasters most of his life. When freights and berths were difficult to come by he, in his younger days, also worked on the land in farming.

Enid at Rolle Quay, Barnstaple 1939

The engine was installed in what was the skipper's cabin aft, who then berthed in the foc'sle, a comfortable v-shape with settees and berths, a table and an iron coal stove for cooking, together with a primus stove.

The food was cooked by the mate and it was eggs and bacon for breakfast and Keillers marmalade with doorsteps of bread. A stewpot was kept going on the stove and anything from rabbits to tinned pineapple was added periodically to top it up. The traditional teapot was kept continually going with more tea added as needed. The "heads" were somewhat primitive in the engine room and washing was in cold water in a bowl on deck drawn from a fresh water drum.

We left the Pill on the tide on the Saturday to motor up the River Taw to Barnstaple where the slag was discharged a basketful at a time. We then came back down the Taw empty to beach the ship on the sand at Crowe Point at the mouth of the Taw. The skipper told me that in his fathers day before engines

were installed when there was no favourable wind, it was commonplace to kedge the ship up the river to Barnstaple, taking several tides to cover the five miles.

All day on the Tuesday we loaded sand from the beach, basket by basket until 6 p.m. The flood tide having made, loading ceased, we battened down the hatch and made ready for sea. By then there was sufficient water to cross Bideford Bar, we up anchored and motored into Bideford Bay on a summer's evening with a light south west force three wind. When clear of the Bar the main, mizzen and jib were set and the engine stopped. With the last of the flood we rounded Baggy and Morte Points and set course for the Mumbles. On a perfect July evening with a full moon we sailed across the Bristol Channel to arrive off the Mumbles at 1 a.m. on the Wednesday where we anchored for the rest of the night. At 6 a.m. to the aroma of frying bacon from the foc'sle it was up anchor and we motored to Neath arriving at our berth at 7.30 a.m. At

Enid with deck cargo of coal in Bristol Channel

Enid – the open wheel

that time it was the skipper's custom to use the engine whenever there was lack of wind or a foul one, only making a passage under sail alone if it was a fair wind. That day with the aid of a mechanical grab the sand was discharged for use in the building trade. We completed unloading by 4 p.m. and proceeded down to the fish wharf at Swansea for the night. After an evening ashore

sampling the South Wales pubs we left at 5 a.m. for Penarth, motor sailing. On our way up the Welsh coast we passed the ketches *Ann* of Salcombe and *Ade* of Barnstaple, motor sailing westwards. By mid morning we were off Barry Harbour and the tide having turned foul, we put in for a few hours to wait for the next flood in our favour. Whilst there, we saw the four-masted barque *Olivebank* soon to be the victim of a German mine in the North Sea and the ketch *Democrat* bound for Barnstaple. Later that day we left for Penarth. To show how many sailing coasters were still in commission in those days, that afternoon we passed the two-masted schooner *Welcombe*, the three-masted schooners *Harold Cairns* and *James Postlethwaite* and the ketches *C.F.H.* and *Garlandstone*. We berthed in Penarth at 7 p.m. and after another evening ashore, we were up early to load washed Lucy Thomas coal. This coming down a chute all hands had to set to, trimming the cargo in the hold. Loading was completed by 11 a.m. and after battening down we sailed for Lynmouth, North Devon. We had an excess of 5 tons of coal which the hold would not accommodate and this was left loose on the deck. By now the wind was a fresh north easterly 4-5 and under sail only we made a fast passage across the Bristol Channel. There was a fairly big sea running and we were taking water aboard which proceeded to wash half the deck cargo overboard. After a wet sail we arrived off Lynmouth at 8 p.m., anchored off and at high water berthed alongside the jetty. Unloading started the next morning and when I left the ship in the afternoon to catch the P and A Campbell paddle steamer *Devonia* for a more sedate passage to Ilfracombe, the ship was ready to sail on the next tide for Braunton so the skipper and mate could be home in time for their Sunday dinner.

Enid, Braunton Pill 1939

This was a typical voyage for the *Enid* in those days. The round trip took 7 to 10 days and whenever possible they worked it to be at home at weekends. The skipper/owner made about £8 a week for himself, after the cost of running the ship and the mates wages were £4 per week, not a bad wage for those days but

Enid in Bristol Channel 1939

the work was hard.

The *Enid* continued to trade until after World War II when I went to sea on her again, but in the late 40's was sold owing to the skippers health and was last heard of going on a world cruise in 1950.

Enid – Skipper and Mate in Bristol Channel

Enid in Bristol Channel taken from *Clara May* 1939

Ann at Vellator

I acknowledge permission from Stan Rogers of the ketch *Acacia* to reproduce this section on trading from Braunton.

BRAUNTON'S CONNECTION WITH THE SEA GOES BACK MANY YEARS.

In the early 1900's many folk were carried in local ships to South Wales to work in the coal mines and steelworks. There were constant crossings of relatives to see these new wonders. 'Emigrants' returning for holidays told of their new-found prosperity. Many made a habit of coming home for Barnstaple Fair. In addition to passengers all kinds of freight were carried. Iron and copper ore were loaded at Combe Martin, Watermouth and Vellator. There is a small quantity of iron ore still left on the quay at Vellator. This came from the mines at Spreacombe. During the summer months there was a considerable trade for small craft carrying limestones and coal from South Wales to various beaches on the North Devon coast. Lime burning was a big industry. There were kilns at Vellator, six at various places on Barnstaple river and others at Croyde, Putsborough and Woolacombe.

Cargoes of barley and pit props and smaller amounts of tin plate boxes, potatoes, carrots and mangolds were loaded at Vellator. The two latter items were for the pit ponies in South Wales. The *Harriet* took the last cargo of carrots from Fremington. Another vessel the *Comet,* took some part cargoes of pottery for Fishleys of Fremington.

With the coming of the railway, Fremington became a very busy place. Thousands of tons of coal were discharged there, as well as timber and basic slag. Many cargoes of clay from the Marland area were loaded from the quay. Part of the original railway bridge was made to open and small vessels were able to pass through to discharge their cargoes in the Pill.

During the summer months many traded

to places on the Cornish coast – Bude, Padstow, Wadebridge, Newquay and St Ives. Ports on the south coast of Cornwall were commonly known as "being round the land" – Cadgwith, Falmouth, Truro and Helford came under this heading. Many of the vessels were owned by the men who sailed them. The masters were given the name of "Captain" but they had no standing.

From Braunton a trip began at the port of discharge. It was a common sight to see men walking to Barnstaple in the early morning to reach their vessels. When empty if there was wind they sailed down the river, but if it was calm they were often towed along by the crew in the boat. This practice was sometimes followed when the vessels were loaded. Some carried sweeps and these were also used in calm weather. Other methods were warping and tracking. Warping was usually carried out with two men in the boat. A kedge carried in the stern with rope attached was pulled away until the order given by the pilot – "heave out". The kedge was then thrown overboard, care being taken to see that it was the right way up. Attached to the crown was a buoy rope with a piece of wood or bunch of corks on the end. This was held by one of the men while the other worked both oars to keep the boat straight ready for the next move. The rope was taken to the hand winch aboard the vessel and wound in. When the distance between the vessel and boat was short the order "weigh away" was given. The kedge was pulled up and the process repeated. The length of warp used varied according to the turns in the channel. The *Acacia* carried a pair of paddles and on occasions when short of help, warping was carried on with one man in the boat. In this event the kedge was carried in the bow. This generally meant that the boat was facing in the right direction for the next move. In both cases speed and skill were necessary.

Tracking was carried out by men on the river bank pulling the vessel along by a rope. Among the places where this happened was along the cutting from Vellator Quay to the toll house, from Barnstaple railway bridge through the drawbridge to Pilton, and on the canal at Lydney.

Payment in those days was by the trip, the same sum whether it took three days, three weeks or even longer. As a rule, gravel was the outward cargo but if there was no demand for this, a few tons of sand were thrown in as ballast. In some cases this was taken out free depending on the place of loading. At other times it had to be thrown overboard. There was no pay for master or crew in either case.

Hundreds of cargoes of gravel were taken from Crow to help build the docks at Swansea, Barry, Cardiff, Bristol, Newport and Avonmouth. This gravel was also used to build the foundations of the transporter bridge at Newport. Cargoes were taken to all the small ports from Ilfracombe to Gloucester. Cargoes brought back to Braunton and Barnstaple were coal, salt, manure, basic slag, grain, flour, timber, bricks, tiles, pipes, cement, slates and cracked stones. In 1854 the *John and Ann* brought as part of her cargo three recast and two new bells for Pilton Church.

Vellator was once a very busy place especially on spring tides. At times there were three vessels discharging coal for various merchants. This was often retailed direct from the ship. Horses and carts and butts were used. It took two to three days to

Acacia at Vellator

discharge, according to the number of horses available. Many farmers of the district fetched their own coal. The price before 1914 was around £1 a ton.

Freights were low. Vessels were paid 3/6 to 4/- per ton for gravel out of which 8d went to the parish council and Trinity House. Coal from Ely Harbour to Fremington 2/9 to 3/- per ton; Newport to Braunton or Barnstaple 4/-; from Lydney 4/6. Bricks from Bridgwater were carried at an agreed price per 1000. Freights rose during the 1914–18 war but slumped afterwards.

There were two ship repairing yards at Vellator. One was on Wrafton Bank and owned by Mr Fred Clarke. After that closed down another yard on the opposite bank was opened by Messrs W Bray and E Evans. They were very busy for some years fitting auxiliary engines into local vessels and doing general repairs. In the old days the vessels created a great deal of work for W Braund and Sons, sailmakers who had a loft in South Street, Braunton.

At the outbreak of the 1914–18 war, there were probably 150 vessels belonging over The Bar – Braunton and Appledore, as many as 60 going out on one tide. There was great competition to get to the port of discharge first. The time taken varied according to the wind and the capabilities of the various vessels. With a good fair wind it was possible to get to Swansea, Cardiff, Barry or Newport on the same day. Cargoes were taken to various ports in the British Isles. There was a big trade to Ireland, Channel Islands and ports on the Continent. Some of the larger ships went to Spain, Portugal and Iceland. The smaller ketches traded mostly in the Bristol Channel. Coal was taken to places in South Wales like Tenby, Caldy Island, Saundersfoot, Solva and St Davids. Some went on to load cracked stones at Porthgain for Barnstaple R.D.C.

Life was not easy in those days. During the winter when vessels were windbound, sailors and their families found life very hard, the position of wives especially so and they made great sacrifices for their children. There was no unemployment pay and sailors turned their hands to all sorts of odd jobs, especially on the farms when they could not go to sea.

By the end of the 1914–18 war, it became plain that small sailing coasters were doomed. Freights became more difficult to obtain. There was great competition from the railways and later road transport. Gradually the numbers decreased and vessels were sold and used for other purposes. Winter gales took their toll and some were lost, even with all their crew. Vessels which had carried a crew of three now sailed with two and still found it hard to make a living. The advent of oil engines kept some going for a number of years, but they gradually disappeared.

To demonstrate the hazards faced by the ketches the following is an Extract from the Ships' Protest Book of the Port of Barnstaple, Continuation Volume dated September 1886 to April 1899.

TO ALL PEOPLE to whom this Public Instrument of Protest shall come William Henry Toller of Barnstaple in the County of Devon in the Kingdom of Great Britain Notary Public by Royal Authority duly admitted and sworn and a Commissioner to administer Oaths in the Supreme Court of Judicature in England Send Greeting Know ye that on the nineteenth day of October 1891 before me the said Notary at Barnstaple aforesaid personally appeared John Chugg Master of the Ketch or Vessel Two Sisters of Barnstaple of sixty nine tons register laden with a cargo of oats and bound therewith from Kinsale to Poole but then lying within the Port of Barnstaple aforesaid who thereupon noted and entered with me the said Notary his Protest against the seas winds weather and other circumstances which the said Vessel met with and experienced from the time of her sailing from Kinsale aforesaid until her arrival at Ilfracombe aforesaid as hereinafter is particularly mentioned and know ye further that on the sixth day of November instant before me the said Notary at Barnstaple aforesaid again appeared the said John Chugg and also Richard Robbins, mate and John White, seaman of the said vessel and who then and there voluntarily and severally solemnly declared and said that having completed the loading of their said Vessels' Cargo they at about 12 a'noon of the fifteenth day of the month of October last having the wind from the West and fine weather departed from Kinsale aforesaid (at which time she was tight staunch and sound and well and sufficiently masted sailed rigged victualled manned tackled and furnished with all kinds of necessary materials and stores her hatches and masts and pumps well covered and secured and the said vessel in every respect well found and fit for the seas and the voyage she was then about to undertake).

About 8 p.m. on the same day stowed fore stay sail wind increasing with a heavy sea continually breaking on the deck at 10 p.m. lowered mainsail on deck to prevent the sea that was continually breaking on the deck and hatches from breaking in the hatches. Pumps carefully attended to ship's head reaching on starboard tack under double reefed mizen and standing jib. Blowing a hurricane from the south south east with a tremendous sea continually breaking on the decks and hatches flooding the cabin and forecastle. At 2 a.m. a temendous sea struck the ship on the starboard bows throwing her on her beam end and carrying away the jib boom standing jib stay and flooding the decks and cabin. Had to knock away bulwarks to right the ship. Jib boom came alongside and thumping the ship. For the benefit of all concerned had to cut away the jibs and all head gear to try and right the ship and keep the wreckage from staving in the ship's side. Pump carefully attended to at 2.30 a.m. a heavy squall struck the ship carried away the mizen throwing the ship down on her port side and flooding the decks and cabin and forecastle. Pumps carefully attended to the ship making a little water. Had to get gaff top sail in the mizen rigging to keep the ship's head to sea as she was laying in the trough of the sea and the sea making a clean break over her. At 11 a.m. cut away all the remaining gear from the mizen and had to set jib in its place ship running before the gale. Tremendous sea continually breaking on the decks and hatches pumps carefully attended to. About 3 a.m. on the 17th October last sighted Lundy bearing south east ½ east wind west by north blowing a heavy gale and looking threatening. At 9 a.m. abreast Morte Point and decided to run into Ilfracombe Harbour as the ship was not safe to proceed up Channel having a list to port. Arrived at Ilfracombe at 12.30 p.m. at low water ship striking the ground heavily and continued to do so until the tide raised when got out warp and warped ship into the inner harbour. Sounded the pumps and found ship making a little water. On the 23rd October last engaged a steam tug and proceeded to Highbridge and arrived there about 10 p.m. on the 24th October last. Pumps carefully attended throughout.

And all the said appearers did further severally declare and say that all the loss damage and prejudice which the said vessel her masts spars sails rigging cables anchors ropes boats appurtenances and cargo or any or either of them or any part or parts thereof had sustained suffered or received the whole thereof whatsoever was solely owing to or occasioned by or through or in consequence of the said seas winds weather and other the circumstances which she met with and experienced as aforesaid at they apprehended and verily believed and was not as they all positively declared in anywise owing to occasioned by or through or in consequence of any design neglect carelessness mismanagement, or any other default of these appearers or the rest of their said vessels company and all the said appearers did lastly declare that the aforegoing is a correct statement of facts and that they severally make this solemn declaration conscientiously believing the same to be true by virtue of the Statutory Declarations Act 1835 wherefore I the notary public aforesaid at the special instance and request of the several undersigned appearers have protested and by these presents do now protest against the seas winds weather and other circumstances which the said vessel met with and experienced as aforesaid for all loss damage demurrage fall of market detention and prejudice which the said vessel her masts spars sails rigging cables anchors ropes boats furniture appurtenances or the cargo on board her or the owners shippers freighters consigners or underwriters of the said vessel and cargo or any other person or persons whomsoever interested or concerned therein respectively have or hath sustained suffered or received or shall or may sustain suffer or receive from or by reason or means of the premises and especially for the said vessels cargo and gear.

In testimony of the truth whereof I the notary aforesaid have hereunto subsribed my name and set my public and usual notarial seal at Barnstaple aforesaid this sixth day of November one thousand eight hundred and ninety one. John Chugg Richard Robbins   John White

Declared by the said Richard Robbins and John White at Barnstaple in the County of Devon this 6th day of November 1891. W.H. Toller.
Declared by the said John Chugg at Braunton in the County of Devon this 9th day of November 1891. W.H. Toller Notary Public Barnstaple Devon England.

The following is an extract from "Trows of Severn and Wye" produced by Chepstow Museum.

"The trows were sailing barges once common on the River Severn and its navigable tributaries, such as the Wye, the Usk and the Bristol Avon. They were the main form of transport for goods in this area for many centuries. Their importance began to decline in the latter part of the last century due to the more economical use of steam tugs and lighters. By the 1920's there were only a handful of these boats still in use. The first documentary evidence relating to these vessels is to be found in Henry IV's Parliamentary Rolls of 1411, but their origin was probably much earlier than this. It is thought that the name "trow" is derived from the same Anglo Saxon word "trog" or "troh" (trough) because of the trows trough like shape.

This shape, and the trow's overall design developed to meet the characteristics of the River Severn, which river has a tidal range of fifty feet, the second largest in the world. It is also very fast flowing in places with tidal races sometimes reaching speeds of ten knots. Added to this is the Severn Bore (a small tidal wave), and the hazards of numerous shifting sandbanks. The trow was therefore built with rounded bilges and a flat bottom, which sometimes curved upwards in the middle rather than having a fixed keel, so it could go over sand banks at speed when needed for sailing. Other characteristics of the trow were, its fullness in the bows and the run and its open hold. The only parts of the vessel that were decked were sections in the stern and the bows under which were cabins for the master and the crew. This open hold enabled cargo to be heaped very high in the trow. Loading and unloading was made easier by the open sides of the boat, and canvas side cloths were stretched along the side of the vessel in order to protect the cargo in open water. These were later made of wood and called side-boards.

Early trows had square sails rigged on a mast that could be lowered when going under low bridges, a characteristic that continued after the style of rigging was altered. By the mid nineteenth century changes were taking place. Triangular fore and aft sails replaced the old square sails and the trows were rigged either as sloops or as ketches, for greater manoeuverability. Where the trow was not able to sail, for instance on the canals which ran into the Severn, such as the Berkeley Canal, they were

Severn trows *Harriet*, *William* and *Volunteer*

sometimes towed by donkeys.

Hitherto the trows which had plied the Severn to its upper reaches were primarily river craft rarely venturing far into the estuary. By the mid nineteenth century larger trows were being built which could cope with bigger cargoes and with voyages beyond the estuary. These sea going trows were "box" trows as they had decks and hatches over the holds and had built in bulwarks instead of side-boards. The changes in design and lengthening of journeys reflected the competition that the trows were facing from the speedier more reliable railways. For instance it had once been common for trows to sail as far as Shrewsbury, but by 1870 because of railway competition they rarely went further north than Tewkesbury. Similarly, the railway built along the Wye valley in 1873 did much to kill the trows carrying trade on the Wye. To combat this the trow skippers extended their seagoing trade and some sailed as far afield as Ireland, Brittany and Belgium carrying coals from the Forest of Dean. These changes were also influenced by the silting up of rivers and the changing industrial pattern in the area of the South Wales coalfields.

The coalfields carried by the trows were very varied and reflected the large area which they served. Coal from the Forest of Dean was an important cargo from the 16th century but trows also carried iron from Coalbrookdale, exotic spices and wine imported into Bristol, stone from Chepstow quarries and farm produce from the Welsh countryside."

Like the deep water ketches, their numbers steadily declined after World War I until all that was left were a few which became motor barges or lighters. The only surviving trow is the *Spry* built at Chepstow in 1894. She was a lower Severn trow and was in trade in the Bristol Channel and up to Worcester until 1950. Now in the care of the Ironbridge Gorge Museum restoration is being carried out on her.

A.T.

Official number:	104112
Built:	1894 Milford
Builder:	J & W Francis
Owners:	Thomas Thomas, Aberporth, Cardigan
	H Redmore, Braunton
Ports of Registry:	Milford
	Barnstaple
Net Reg Tons:	36
Dimensions:	62.0 x 18.0 x 7.0
Draught	7.1

ACACIA

Official number:	81036
Built:	1880 Plymouth
Builder:	Banks
Owners:	William J Rogers, Braunton
	S. Rogers, Braunton
Signal Letters:	T.D.J.V.
Port of Registry:	Barnstaple
Net Reg Tons:	40
Dimensions:	60.3 x 18.6 x 7.4

First built as a smack. Rerigged as a ketch in 1880's was in the flour trade for many years. Became a barge in S. Wales.

ACTIVE

Official number:	11706
Built:	1811 Bridgnorth
Owner:	J G Sully, Bridgwater
Port of Registry:	Bridgwater
Net Reg Tons:	64

A Severn trow schooner rigged.

ADA

Official number:	62742
Built:	1869 Bristol
Owners:	T Gardner, Gloucester
	A Johns, Gloucester
Port of Registry:	Gloucester
Net Reg Tons:	67

Dismasted in the Bristol Channel in June 1929. Towed to Highbridge   by a steamer. Hulked at Purton 1951.

A Seven trow.

ADA

Official number:	22736
Built:	1844 Padstow
Owners:	W Rundle, St Blazey
	Arthur Goldsworthy, Appledore
Port of Registry:	Bideford
Net Reg Tons:	38

ADE (formerly *Annie Christian)*

Official number:	76819
Built:	1881 Barnstaple
Builder:	William Westacot
Owners:	Isaac Allen, Watchet
	Ayre, Braunton
	1882 E Quay, C Ramsey
	1885-1889 D Shaw, Garleston
	1913 Somerset Trading Co
	1920 L M Bowerman, Bridgwater
	1929 P K Harris, Appledore
Signal Letters:	J.C.F.H.
Ports of Registry:	Barnstaple
	Bridgwater
	Bideford
	Liverpool
Net Reg Tons:	69
Dimensions:	76.5 x 20.5 x 9.0

First rigged as a schooner, rerigged as a ketch in 1894. Sunk in collision 1888 raised and redecked. Had a small gun on foredeck during Great War. Motor installed in 1916. Broken up Appledore 1946. Her hulk lies on the shore. At one time named *Sunshine*.

ADVANCE

Official number:	999999
Built:	1893 Pembroke
Builder:	J W Francis
Owners:	A Graham, Saundersfoot
	Mrs A Graham Incledon, Braunton
Signal Letters:	N.F.K.H.
Port of Registry:	Milford
Net Reg Tons:	59
Dimensions:	71.7 x 19.3 x 8.6
Draught:	9.5

ADVENTURE

Official number:	5630
Built:	1834 Plymouth
Owner:	E Hamblin, Bridgwater
Signal Letters:	J.K.M.G.
Port of Registry:	Bridgwater
Net Reg. Tons:	55

AILSIE (Formerly *Rob Roy)*

Official number:	86123
Built:	1882 Porthleven
Owner:	J Mead, Falmouth
Signal Letters:	H.J.T.P.
Pot of Registry:	Falmouth
Net Reg Tons:	23

Agnes. Stranded Ireland 1919

AGNES
(Formerly *Lady Acland & Margaret Francis*)

Official number:	105246
Built:	1830 Upper Canal Basin, Bude
Rebuilt:	1903 Bude
Builder:	Stapleton
Rebuilder:	Rudland Brothers
Owners:	O Davy, Bude
	N H Tregaskes, Bude
	H Clarke, Braunton & Mitchell
	Peter Herbert, Bude
	A Barr
Port of Registry:	Bideford
Net Reg Tons:	54
Gross Tons:	67
Dimensions:	70.6 x 18.5 x 8.0
	Lengthened by 3' when rebuilt

Plied on the coal trade between S Wales and Cornish ports. Fitted out for a voyage to Australia in 1957. Wrecked in a hurricane in the West Indies probably at Barbados. Beached on a reef and broke up.

Agnes at the Pill, Braunton 1945

Agnes at the Pill, Braunton 1939

Agnes loading wheat feed at Barry 1955

19

ALBATROSS

Official number:	26761
Built:	1851 Honey St Wilts
Owners:	W Hickery, Bristol
	J Rogers, Hanham
Port of Registry:	Bristol
Net Reg Tons:	36

First rigged as a sloop.

ALBERT (Formerly *St Marie*)

Official number:	60741
Built:	
Owner:	A Nicholas, Watchet
Signal Letters:	J.F.Q.R.
Port of Registry:	Plymouth
Net Reg Tons:	46
Gross Tons:	80

ALERT

Official number:	69919
Built:	1867 Saul
Rebuilt:	1877
Owner:	J A Streetly, Clevedon
Port of Registry:	Gloucester
Net Reg Tons:	34

A sloop rigged Severn trow.

ALFORD

Official number:	79357
Built:	1885 Bideford
Builder:	H M Restarick
Owners:	A Nicholas, Watchet
	J W Banbury, Bude
Signal Letters:	H.N.D.F.
Port of Registry:	Bideford
Net Reg Tons:	66
Dimensions:	77.5 x 19.7 x 7.8
Draught:	8.5

There is some evidence that she was originally built in 1835. Lost in gale on Dutch coast whilst on passage to Hamburg September 1922. Traded far afield to London, Plymouth, Cork, Garston, Ipswich and S Wales carrying manure, wood, salt, china clay, coal and many other cargoes including lime and grain.

ALFRED & EMMA

Official number:	27691
Built:	1861 Pembroke Dock
Owners:	J S Cunningham, Isle of Man
	H Clarke, Braunton
Port of Registry:	Barnstaple
Net Reg Tons:	58

First rigged as a schooner. Rerigged as a ketch in 1880's. Stranded Saunton Sands April 1922.

ALICE

Official number:	47963
Built:	1868 Chepstow
Owners:	T Sargent Chepstow
	D Gower, Cardiff
Rebuilt:	1896
Port of Registry:	Bristol
Net Reg Tons:	76

ALICE

Official number:	93437
Built:	1890 Milford Haven
Owner:	H Davies, Cardigan
Port of Registry:	Milford
Net Reg Tons:	30

ALMA

Official number:	11684
Built:	1854 Gloucester
Owner:	A J Smith, Bristol
Signal Letters:	K.T.F.V.
Port of Registry:	Gloucester
Net Reg Tons:	54
Dimensions:	77 x 17 x 6

A half boxed Severn trow. Rebuilt 1916. In trade until 1939. Became a barge in Bristol 1943.

ALPHA

Official number:	63504
Built:	1870 Truro
Builder:	Charles Dyer
Owners:	C Kelway, W Penrose, John Eastick & Joseph Hunkin, Truro
	W K Slade (1897-1912), Appledore
	John Cox, Appledore
Signal Letters:	J.M.D.Q.
Port of Registry:	Bideford
Net Reg Tons:	55
Dimensions:	75.2 x 19.3 x 8.8

First rigged as a schooner and traded to Newfoundland. Rerigged as a ketch 1897. Motor installed 1924. Sank in Bideford Bay 1933.

ALWYN

Official number:	86526
Built:	1885 Plymouth
Builder:	Watson & Fox
Owners:	C A Fox, Plymouth
	James Mead, Appledore
Port of Registry:	Bideford
Net Reg Tons:	67
Dimensions:	73.2 x 19.3 x 9.1
Draught:	9.9

AMAZON

Official number:	55266
Built:	1886 Jersey
Builder:	Le Sueur
Owners:	Mrs B Watts, Braunton
	James Watts, Braunton
Ports of Registry:	Hull
	Barnstaple
Net Reg Tons:	50
Dimensions:	65.5 x 16.3 x 8.2
Draught:	8.9

Lost Plymouth 1936.

AMY

Official number:	97940
Built:	1890 Blyth
Owner:	T Stooke, Exmouth
	J. Crick, Braunton
Signal Letters:	L.P.K.R.
Port of Registry:	Newcastle
Net Reg Tons:	51

ANN (Formerly *Bonnie Brown*)

Official number:	10881
Built:	1805 Dartmouth
Owner:	R Allen, Bridgwater
Signal Letters:	K.Q.H.V.
Port of Registry:	Bridgwater
Net Reg Tons:	54
Gross Tons:	100

ANN

Official number:	11671
Built:	1814 Bowes Yard, Salop
Owner:	G Wheatstone, Bristol
Signal Letters:	K.T.P.B.
Port of Registry:	Bristol
Net Reg Tons:	54

A Severn trow.

ANN

Official number:	86469
Built:	1889 Kingsbridge
Builder:	D Date
Owners:	W E Hurdle, Topsham
	Thomas A Slee, Braunton
	C Chugg, Braunton
Port of Registry:	Salcombe
Net Reg Tons:	47

Used to work the beach at Combe Martin, N Devon. Reduced to hulk and beached Swansea. Fitted with 15 b.h.p. engine in 1920's.

Ann at Lynmouth 1928

ANNE

Official number:	63099
Built:	1873 Hempstead, Gloucester
Owner:	William S Moreland, Hempstead
Signal Letters:	M.P.T.V.
Port of Registry:	Gloucester
Net Reg Tons:	88

ANNIE

Official number:	65158
Built:	1872 Barnstaple
Builder:	W Westacott
Owners:	H Fimmore, Plymouth
	Luisa Le Gros, Cardiff
Ports of Registry:	Bideford
	Jersey
Net Reg Tons:	58
Dimensions:	75.0 x 19.5 x 18.8
Draught:	9.10

First rigged as a schooner.

ANNIE

Official number:	104117
Built:	1896 Milford Haven
Builder:	J W Francis
Owner:	H Jones, Pembroke
Ports of Registry:	Cardigan
	Milford
Dimensions:	64.5 x 18.1 x 7.0
Net Reg Tons:	32
Gross Tons:	46

Carried grain from Avonmouth to Cornish ports and also traded to Irish ports.

ANNIE

Official number:	93438
Built:	1890 Galampton
Owner:	G Rowe, Tenby
Net Reg Tons:	23
Port of Registry:	Milford

ANNIE DAVEY

Official number:	67651
Built:	1873 Bude
Builder:	Stapleton
Owners:	O Davey, Bude
	H Stapleton, Bude
Signal Letters:	L.P.G.Q.
Port of Registry:	Bideford
Net Reg Tons:	63

Once blown by blizzard into Bay of Biscay whilst on passage with coal Saundersfoot to Ipswich. Lost in collision off Sussex coast.

ANT

Official number:	11492
Built:	1810 Fowey
Owners:	H Stapleton, Bude
	J H Hooper, Bude
Port of Registry:	Bideford
Net Reg Tons:	49

Lost in collision 1895 whilst bound Isle of Wight to Efford with cement.

ANT

Official number:	43671
Built:	1861 Gloucester
Owners:	W G Camp, Bristol
	J Nott, Newport
Port of Registry:	Bristol
Net Reg Tons:	47

ARABELLA

Official number:	47746
Built:	1864 Saul
Owners:	C Saul, Gloucester
	O Cam, Saul
Port of Registry:	Gloucester
Net Reg Tons:	70

Wrecked on Brittons Rock, Ilfracombe 1895. A Severn trow.

Ant in Bude Canal after being lengthened from a smack

ARGO

Official number:	56366
Built:	1868 Swansea
Builder:	Robert Vanstone
Owners:	Lewis Lewday, Appledore
	J Ridler, Porlock
	H Pulsford, Porlock
Port of Registry:	Bideford
Net Reg Tons:	41

First rigged as a smack. Converted to ketch rig in 1880's.

ARGO

Official number:	11628
Built:	1833 Stourport
Owners:	E Spurway, Bridgwater
	T R Brown, Knowle, Somerset
Signal Letters:	K.T.L.D.
Port of Registry:	Gloucester
	Bridgwater
Net Reg Tons:	69
Dimensions:	62.0 x 17.8 x 7.9

ARK

Official number:	63086
Built:	1871 Framilode
Owner:	Howell G Bryant, Bridgwater
Port of Registry:	Gloucester
Net Reg Tons:	55

Trade from Lydney and Cardiff to Bridgwater with coal. A ketch rigged Severn trow.

ARK

Official number:	10811
Built:	1841 Wilton, Cheshire
Owner:	J G Sully, Wembton, Somerset
Port of Registry:	Bridgwater
Net Reg Tons:	66

A Severn trow. Survived as a barge until the 1930's.

ARTHUR

Official number:	74713
Built:	1876 Southtown
Builder:	H Fellows & Son
Owners:	W Brown, Southtown
	Richard Bound, Bridgwater
Signal Letters:	Q.S.G.J.
Port of Registry:	Bridgwater
Net Reg Tons:	54
Dimensions:	74.0 x 18.3 x 8.0

Mostly traded with bricks from Bridgwater to Ireland. Broken up 1926.

ATLAS

Official number:	45720
Built:	1864 Bristol
Owners:	O T Camm, Saul
	W Gibson, Bristol
Port of Registry:	Bristol
Net Reg Tons:	58

AURORA

Official number:	22978
Built:	1817 Brixham
Owners:	W Blackmore, Fremington
	John Butler, Appledore
	James Cook, Appledore
Signal Letters:	N.P.R.T.

First rigged as a schooner.

A.T. leaving Bude 1938

AURORA

Official number:	77357
Built:	1877 Port Mellon
Owners:	P Hankin, Mevagissey
	H G Norman, Watchet
Port of Registry:	Bridgwater
Net Reg Tons:	36
Dimensions:	76.5 x 16.6 x 6.7

Whilst bound Caernarvon to Southampton August 1929 went ashore at Hayle and broke up. Abandoned in Swansea and seized by authorities in 1924.

Ketch *Ark* and *Fannie Jane* at Parret river, Bridgwater

AURORA

Official number:	87604
Built:	1883 Gloucester
Owner:	W H Butler, St Georges, Bristol
Port of Registry:	Gloucester
Net Reg Tons:	42

A Severn trow.

AUSPICIOUS

Official number:	4026
Built:	1822 Bristol
Owners:	J Pollard, Porlock
	R Tancock, Weston Super Mare
Signal Letters:	H.W.R.J.
Port of Registry:	Barnstaple
Net Reg Tons:	47

Built as a pilot cutter. Became the Weston Super Mare coal boat.

AVON

Official number:	15222
Built:	1856 Aldermaston
Owner:	F Hawkins, Bristol
Signal Letters:	L.R.J.S.
Net Reg Tons:	29
Port of Registry:	Bristol

A Severn trow.

AVON

Official number:	65307
Built:	1871 Crew Hole, Gloucestershire
Owner:	T Stone, Bristol
Port of Registry:	Bristol
Net Reg Tons:	22

A sloop rigged Severn trow.

AVON

Official number:	21194
Built:	1858 Bristol
Owner:	Severn & Canal Carrying Co, Gloucester
Port of Registry:	Bristol
Net Reg tons:	65

A Severn trow.

AUSPICIOUS

Official number:	13428
Built:	1833 Appledore
Builder:	William Clibbett
Owner:	T Gough, Falmouth
Port of Registry:	Falmouth
Net Reg Tons:	54

Lengthened 1850 first rigged as a schooner.

Bessie – deck view

BESSIE

Official number:	112455
Built:	1900 Milford
Builder:	J W Francis
Owners:	J G Trevine, Pembroke
	F Incledon & Clarke, Braunton
	A Chugg, Braunton
Port of Registry:	Barnstaple
Net Reg Tons:	34
Dimensions:	59.4 x 18.0 x 6.6
Draught:	7.4

Sold foreign in 1946 and went to South of France and later to Famagusta.

Schooner *Result,* a ketch *Bessie,* Vellator 1939

Bessie Clarke at Braunton Pill

BEATRICE HANNAH

Official number:	93456
Built:	1888 Bridgwater
Owners:	J Nurse, Epney
	Mrs M H Nurse, Stonehouse
Port of Registry:	Gloucester
Net Reg Tons:	68

BERNARD

Official number:	114045
Built:	1904 Knottingley
Builder:	J Cartick & Son
Owner:	G Armitage, Rothwell
Signal Letters:	W.B.M.F.
Port of Registry:	Goole
Net Reg Tons:	59
Dimensions:	73.6 x 17.8 x 8.4

Mostly traded with bricks from Bridgwater to Irish ports. Foundered 1930.

BERNARD BARTON

Official number:	8642
Built:	1840 Woodbridge
Owners:	T K Ridler, Porlock
	W Trott, Woodbridge
	E Pasiful, Woodbridge
Signal Letters:	K.D.B.T.
Port of Registry:	Woodbridge
Net Reg Tons:	97
Dimensions:	79.3 x 19.5 x 10.2

Lost off Lundy Island 1899. First rigged as a schooner.

BERTIE

Official number:	69406
Built:	1877 Bridgwater
Owners:	R Davey, Totterdown
	E Perkins, West Porlock
Signal Letters:	R.B.H.Q.
Net Reg Tons:	68
Port of Registry:	Bristol

BESSIE CLARK

Official number:	84471
Built:	1881 Bideford
Builder:	H M Restarick
Owners:	G H Clark, Braunton
	G Gould, Clark, Braunton
Port of Registry:	Barnstaple
Net Reg Tons:	44
Dimensions:	59.1 x 18.2 x 7.5
Gross Tons:	46

First owned Braunton ketch to be fitted with an engine a Fairbanks Morse in 1909. Reputed to be the last ketch to be tiller steered. Plied between South Wales and Cornwall in the lime and coal trade. Was used in 1939-45 war on degaussing and balloon barrage service. Broken up at Cleave Houses, Appledore after war service and her hulk lies on the shore.

Bessie Clark at the Pill, Braunton 1939

Bessie Ellen at Bideford Quay 1945

BESSIE ELLEN

Official number:	120098
Built:	1907 Plymouth
Bulder:	W S Kelly
Owners:	John S Chichester, Braunton
	Mrs B S Chichester, Braunton 1920–46
Signal Letters:	H.K.C.M.
Port of Registry:	Barnstaple
Net Reg Tons:	60
Gross Tons:	78
Dimensions:	77.4 x 20.1 x 9.5

Fitted with 25 h.p. Widdop engine 1916. Salvaged from the wreck Heatherbell. Was in coal trade Lydney and Newport to Appledore and Lyme Regis. Gravel to South Wales and limestone to Plymouth. Ran up on Morte Stone 1910. Salvaged and repaired at Appledore. Sold to Danish Government in 1946 who put in a poop deck, new deck and wheelhouse. Became a motor barge. Later sold to a Mr Petersen and last reported to have been resold to Danish interests in 1983 and at Troense, renamed Forsoget and being extensively rebuilt.

BESSIE GOULD

Official number:	68197
Built:	1872 Barnstaple
Builder:	W Westacott
Owners:	G Chugg, Braunton
	G Clarke, Braunton
Port of Registry:	Barnstaple
Net Reg tons:	48
Dimensions:	65.0 x 20.5 x 8.2

First rigged as a smack. Fitted with engine 1914. Broken up at Appledore 1939.

BESSIE WILKINSON

Official number:	67655
Built:	1874 Appledore
Buider:	Richard Blackmore, Bideford
Owner:	P Wilkinson, Appledore
Port of Registry:	Bideford
Net Reg. Tons:	46

BLACK ROCK

Official number:	27330
Built:	1855 Aldermaston
Owner:	F Hawkins, Bristol
Signal Letters:	P.Q.T.W.
Net Reg Tons:	25
Port of Registry:	Bristol

A Severn trow.

BLUEBELL (Formerly *Union*)

Official number:	27278
Built:	France
Owners:	William Darke, Newquay
	R Norman, Watchet
Signal Letters:	P.Q.N.K.
Port of Registry:	Padstow
Net Reg Tons:	62
Dimensons:	67.1 x 20.4 x 8.6

First rigged as a schooner.

BOCONNOC

Official number:	8641
Built:	1836 Fowey
Owners:	J George, Bude
	J J Sully, Newport
Port of Registry:	Padstow
Net Reg Tons:	37

First rigged as a smack.

BONITA

Official number:	76278
Built:	1881 Jersey
Builder:	D Le Sueur
Owners:	Norman Watchett
	Reuben Chichester, Braunton
Signal Letters:	W.D.C.R.
Ports of Registry:	Jersey
	Barnstaple
Net Reg Tons:	37
Dimensions:	57.9 x 16.1 x 7.4
Draught:	8.0

Whilst on passage to Gloucester with sand lost mainmast in gale in June 1931. The last ketch to carry coal to Lynmouth. Wrecked off Brixie Point near Barry 1937.

BONITO *(Fiducia Dei)*
Official number:	91403
Built:	1885 Beverley
Owner:	Thomas Hutchings, Appledore
Signal Letters:	S.F.C.R.
Port of Registry:	Bideford
Net Reg Tons:	65

Built as a North Sea trawler and converted for cargo carrying.

BRISTOL PACKET
Official number:	16935
Built:	1857 Newport
Owners:	G R Kirsey, Appledore
	J Evans, Appledore
	W J Lord, Appledore
	T Fishwick, Appledore
	J Slade, Appledore 1899–1902
Port of Registry:	Newport
Net Reg Tons:	53

First rigged as a smack. Condemned after damage at Porth Luney Cove, Cornwall and broken up 1916.

BRISTOL PACKET
Official number:	4068
Built:	1827 Tewkesbury
Owners:	C Cam, Arlingham
	T R Brown, Bristol
Signal Letters:	H.W.V.D.
Port of Registry:	Gloucester
Net Reg tons:	49

A Severn trow.

BRACKLEY
Official number:	16403
Built:	1854 Runcorn
Owners:	Brundit, Runcorn
	J S Davies, Runcorn
Port of Registry:	Liverpool
Net Reg Tons:	64

BROTHERS
Official number:	10808
Built:	1847 Brimscombe
Owners:	D Gower, Cardiff
	R & J Rowles, Clevedon
Signal Letters:	K.Q.B.M.
Port of Registry:	Gloucester
Net Reg Tons:	53

A Severn trow.

BRUNSWICK
Official number:	15504
Built:	1833 Bideford
Builder:	George Crocker
Owners:	W Blackmore, Fremington
	J Butler, Bickington
Signal Letters:	L.S.N.M.
Port of Registry:	Bideford
Net Reg Tons:	72

First rigged as a schooner later rerigged as a ketch.

BUTTERCUP
Official number:	67847
Built:	1884 Goole
Builder:	G W Outwin
Owners:	S Babson, Exeter
	Capt. Benny, Falmouth
Signal Letters:	J.P.W.H.
Port of Registry:	Goole
	Falmouth
Net Reg Tons:	89
Dimensions:	78.3 x 20.3 x 10.2
Draught:	9.10

C.F.H. off Penarth 1939

C.F.H.
Official number:	99268
Built:	1892 Calstock
Builder:	J Goss
Owners:	C F Hobson
	H G Clarke, Braunton
	W Hanley, Plymouth
	Capt. Stribling, Braunton
Signal Letters:	N.V.H.K.
Port of Registry:	Barnstaple
Net Reg Tons:	56
Gross Tons:	76
Dimensions:	74.0 x 20.4 x 9.3

C.F.H. at Appledore 1945

First registered Plymouth but sold to French owners and renamed Yolande. Bought by Clarke in 1914 and became C.F.H. again. Traded between France and South Wales with pit props. Motor installed 1914. Fleet tender during Great War at Scapa Flow and supply ship to R.N. 1939–45. Her hulk lies on the Severn below Upton on Severn.

CAERLEON
Official number:	8732
Built:	1820 Newport
Owners:	R Red, Porlock
	J Edwards, Bridgwater
	Wm York, Bridgwater
Ports of Registry:	Bridgwater
	Milford
Net Reg Tons:	40
Dimensions:	50.11 x 17.10 x 7.10

CAMBRIA
Official number:	18356
Built:	1851 Llanelly
Owners:	Mrs E Gates, Pembrokeshire
	F & J Chichester, Braunton
	Mrs E Chichester, Braunton
Signal Letters:	M.L.K.R.
Port of Registry:	Barnstaple
Net Reg Tons:	39

CAROLINE
Official number:	13873
Built:	1824 Plymouth
Owners:	Luke & Co., Fowey
	P K Harris, Appledore
Signal Letters:	L.J.S.T.
Port of Registry:	Bideford
Net Reg Tons:	50

First rigged as a schooner

CAROLINE
Official number:	26762
Built:	1830 Framilode
Owners:	S Rowles, Frampton on Severn
	W R Wallbridge, Cardiff
Signal Letters:	P.M.L.C.
Port of Registry:	Cardiff
Net Reg tons:	53

A Severn trow.

CATHERINE
Official number:	56405
Built:	1869 Llym Bwtri
Builder:	H Jones
Owners:	J Hooper, Appledore
	W. Lamey, Appledore
Signal Letters:	W.J.F.M.
Port of Registry:	Bideford
Net Reg Tons:	50
Dimensions:	75.0 x 19.6 x 8.8

CERES
Official number:	15560
Built:	1811 Salcombe
Owner:	W W Petherick, Bude
Port of Registry:	Dartmouth
	Padstow
Net Reg Tons:	44
Dimensions:	65.2 x 17.7 x 17.2

Originally a fruit smack trading between England and Spain and a store vessel during the Peninsular War. Became Bude owned 1852 and remained in the Petherick family until her loss off Baggy Point in North Devon in 1936, when she was the oldest deep sea ketch in commission. She was lengthened and rerigged as a ketch in 1869. Engine fitted 1913. Capt Walter Petherick was skipper for 52 years. In 1900 went ashore Padstow but was successfully salvaged by a tug. Calculated she carried some 250,000 tons of cargo in 125 years of trading.

CHAMPION
Official number:	10814
Built:	1853 Bristol
Owners:	D Nurse, Bridgwater
	J C Hunt, Bridgwater
Port of Registry:	Bridgwater
Net Reg Tons:	68
Dimensions:	82.7 x 19.2 x 7.9

Broken up 1939.

Ceres

CHARLOTTE

Official number:	11002
Built:	1840 Plymouth
Owners:	W Pickard, Appledore
	P K Harris, Appledore
Signal Letters:	K.Q.T.J.
Port of Registry:	Bideford
Net Reg Tons:	39

First rigged as a smack. Converted to a lighter 1913.

CHARLOTTE

Official number:	47989
Built:	1864 Southampton
Owners:	Wansborough Paper Co., Watchet
	Butler, Braunton
	Davis, Watchet
Signal Letters:	V.Q.W.F.
Port of Registry:	Goole
Net Reg Tons:	69
Gross Tons:	140

CHARLOTTE

Official number:	47233
Built:	1863 Kingston, Sussex
Owners:	J Jenkin, Newquay
	J Neal, Padstow
Signal Letters:	V.M.R.S.
Port of Registry:	Padstow
Net Reg Tons:	62

Wrecked Clovelly 1895.

CICELIA

Official number:	55289
Built:	1867 Jersey
Builder:	Le Suer
Owners:	F & A Bennett, Ilfracombe
	J H Tope, Ilfracombe
Signal Letters:	H.P.G.T.
Port of Registry:	Guernsey
Net Reg Tons:	79
Dimensions:	78.3 x 19.0 x 8.8
Draught:	9.7
Owners:	F & A Bennett, Ilfracombe, 1922-1935

Wrecked off St Ives 1935.
In her early years in the dried cod trade from Newfoundland.

Clara May at The Pill, Braunton 1939

CLARA MAY

Official number:	99255
Built:	1891 Millbay Dock, Plymouth
Builder:	Watson & Fox
Owners:	J B Cornish, Bude
	J Merrifield, Feock
	J Reed, Yeovil
	T & J Hitchcock, Lavenham
	A Parkhouse & Clarke, Braunton
Signal Letters:	R.B.K.D.
Port of Registry:	Plymouth
Net Reg Tons:	69
Gross Tons:	72.5
Dimensions:	75.9 x 19.7 x 8.9
Depth in hold:	8.11

50 h.p. semi diesel installed 1926. Traded until 1953 when broken up at Braunton Pill. Often referred to as Jimmy Cornish's Yacht.

CLARA FELICIA

Official number:	70296
Built:	1873 Nevin
Owners:	R Evans, Portmadoc
	William Holding, Bridgwater
Signal Letters:	M.V.H.C.
Net Reg Tons:	90
Ports of Registry:	Caernarvon
	Bridgwater
Dimensions:	75.0 x 21.0 x 11.3

Wrecked Padstow 1906.

CLAREEN

Official number:	86521
Built:	1884 Plymouth
Owners:	A C Nurse, Bridgwater
	J D Nurse, Bridgwater
Signal Letters:	J.T.P.W.
Port of Registry:	Bridgwater
Net Reg Tons:	78

In collision Milford Haven February 1923. Carried away both masts. Went ashore Waterford Harbour September 1924.

COMET

Official number:	13892
Built:	1842 Guernsey
Owners:	H. Redmore, Braunton
	W Bailey, Southwick
Signal Letters:	L.J.V.C.
Port of Registry:	Southampton
Net Reg Tons:	59
Dimensions:	66.8 x 16.7 x 8.2

Lost off Lands End 1891.

CONSERVATOR

Official number:	19216
Built:	1843 Padstow
Owners:	P Burgess, Lynmouth
	Mrs E Stevens, Mumbles
Signal Letters:	M.R.C.B.
Ports of Registry:	Padstow
	Caernarvon
	Aberystwyth
Net Reg. Tons:	28
Dimensions:	50.3 x 14.9 x 7.0

Lost in collision Bristol Channel 1890. First rigged as a sloop.

CORNFLOWER

Official number:	48874
Built:	1865 Poole
Ownrs:	J M Cox, Appledore
	T Belben, Poole
Signal Letters:	W.V.N.Q.
Port of Registry:	Bideford
Net Reg Tons:	48

CORONATION

Official number:	15575
Built:	
Owner:	J Cook, Bude
Port of Registry:	Bideford
Net Reg tons:	42

Wrecked Roads Point Queenstown 1872 whilst on passage Padstow to Cork.

CORNISH LASS

Official number:	14032
Built:	1841 Padstow
Builder:	A Tredwen
Owner:	J Hitchens, St Agnes
Ports of Registry:	St Ives
	Padstow
Net Reg Tons:	60

Wrecked 1896 entering St Agnes with coal from Lydney.

CROWN OF DENMARK

(Ex Auto. Ex Afienda Marchiena)

Official number:	145111
Built:	1918 Stadskanaal, Holland
Owners:	W Hunt, Braunton
	R Cruikshank, Liverpool
Signal Letters:	K.H.Q.S.
Port of Registry:	London
Gross Tons:	136
Dimensions:	101.6 x 19.1 x 8.5

Built as a schooner and later converted to ketch rig. Was in cement trade between Isle of Wight and Topsham. Sold after World War II to Danish owners. Renamed *Dejro* and reported lying in Copenhagen in the late 1960's in poor repair.

Crown of Denmark at Barnstaple 1939

CROWPILL (Ex *John Wesley*)

Official number:	67524
Built:	1873 Harwich
Owners:	J S White & Co, Cowes
	Sully & Co, Bridgwater
Ports of Registry:	Cowes
	Bridgwater
Net Reg Tons:	184
Dimensions:	94.3 x 24.4 x 11.1

Lost by fire whilst on passage Bridgwater to Lydney. Later used as a towing barge. Believed finished her days as a hulk at Cowes.

CRUISER

Official number:	47890
Built:	1866 Watermouth
Builder:	Wat Symons
Owner:	A C Bassett, Watermouth
Port of Registry:	Barnstaple
Net Reg Tons:	33

Originally sloop rigged. Lengthened and converted to ketch rig by Westacott, Barnstaple 1881. Sank in Channel 1897.

D.P.T.

Official number:	60097
Built:	1868 Dartmouth
Owners:	R B Triplett, Plymouth
	J Hooper, Appledore
Port of Registry:	Bideford
Net Reg tons:	39

DAISY

Official number:	67840
Built:	1883 Goole
Builder:	G W Outwin
Owners:	D Cawthore, Nottingley
	A Lamey, Appledore
Signal Letters:	H.V.R.J.
Port of Registry:	Goole
	Jersey
Net Reg Tons:	65
Dimensions:	76.2 x 19.6 x 9.1

Collision with steamer off Portishead April 1931. Made Lydney for repairs. Became hulk at Uphill, Weston Super Mare and sold for scrap 1938 for £5.

DARING

Official number:	29843
Built:	1863 Bideford
Builder:	Johnson
Owners:	Chas W Price, Newport
	J Slade, Appledore 1921-27
Signal Letters:	O.H.J.M.
Ports of Registry:	Cowes
	Bideford
Net Reg Tons:	48
Dimensions:	68.0 x 18.0 x 9.0

First rigged as a dandy.

DAVID

Official number:	10891
Buit:	1836 Lydney
Owner:	Henry L Smith, Arlingham, Gloucester
Port of Registry:	Bridgwater
Net Reg Tons:	50
Dimensions:	73.1 x 17.0 x 6.2

Schooner rigged Severn trow. Broken up 1934.

DERBY

Official number:	10306
Built:	1839 Bath
Owners:	J Good, Frampton on Severn
	W F Cook, Frampton on Severn
Signal Letters:	K.M.W.B.
Port of Registry:	Bristol
Net Reg Tons:	44

Daisy

DEMOCRAT

Official number:	120099
Built:	1909 Castle Pill, Milford
Owners:	S G Clarke, Braunton
	T & G Welch, Braunton
Port of Registry:	Barnstaple
Net Reg Tons:	43
Dimensions:	71.2 x 19.0 x 7.7
Draught:	8.4

About 1950 carried the last cargo of coal to Porlock. Motor 80 b.h.p. Lost off French coast March 1954 on passage Appledore to Jersey. Sister ship to *Edith*.

DEVON

Official number:	291
Built:	1823 Topsham
Builder:	
Owners:	P Varwell, St Thomas
	J Butler, Bickington
Signal Letters:	H.C.G.L.
Port of Registry:	Barnstaple
Net Reg Tons:	79

First rigged as a schooner.

DEWI WYN

Official number:	1083
Built:	1852 Portmadoc
Owners:	R Rowlands, Bangor
	Mrs L A Guard, Appledore
Signal Letters:	H.G.N.D.
Port of Registry:	Bideford
Net Reg Tons:	49

Foundered Bideford Bay 1911.

DIDO C (Formerly *Jules Claes*)

Official number:	148211
Built:	1921 Lysckil, Sweden
Owner:	S Chugg, Braunton
Port of Registry:	Barnstaple
Net Reg Tons:	41

Ran up on Morte Stone 1936 but got off with little damage. Sold to Scottish owners and sank Ardrossan 1947 after collision. Set alight 1964.

Dido C at Vellator 1939

DILIGENT

Official number:	81028
Built:	1879 Stonehouse
Owner:	E G Bryant, Mevagissey
Port of Registry:	Plymouth
Net Reg Tons:	15

DISPATCH

Official number:	1678
Built:	1852 Barnstaple
Builder:	J Goss
Owners:	Paddison, Braunton
	John Cox, Appledore
Port of Registry:	Barnstaple
Net Reg Tons:	36

First built as a smack and converted to a ketch rig in 1880's.

Dido C on Morte Stone

DOLPHIN

Official number:	45271
Built:	1862 Jersey
Owners:	T S Owen, Appledore
	W Jewell, Appledore
Port of Registry:	Bideford
Net Reg. Tons:	46

DUKE OF CORNWALL

Official number:	19320
Built:	1848 Bideford
Owners:	J Vivian, Penzance
	W Stevens, St Ives
Signal Letters:	M.R.K.W.
Port of Registry:	Penzance
Net Reg Tons:	55

Built as a schooner later rerigged as a ketch.

DUKE OF WELLINGTON

Official number:	4046
Built;	1840 Stourport
Builder:	Russell & Corbett
Owners:	H Hobbs, Bridgwater
	Walter B Trunks, Bridgwater
Ports of Registry:	Bridgwater
	Bristol
Net Reg Tons:	54
Dimensions:	70.6 x 15.9 x 5.6

A Severn trow. A decked trow which at one time traded to Antwerp and Glasgow.

EDGAR

Official number:	63084
Built:	1870 Saul
Owners:	O Cam, Saul
	Mrs E Cam, Saul
Port of Registry:	Gloucester
Net Reg Tons:	70

A Severn trow.

EDITH

Official number:	121611
Built:	1906 Castle Quay, Milford
Owner:	H G Clarke, Braunton
Port of Registry:	Barnstaple
Net Reg Tons:	41
Gross Tons:	55
Dimensions:	67.4 x 18.9 x 7.6

Engine fitted 1910. Run down off Newport salvaged and subsequently sunk in collision in Bristol Channel.

EDITH

Official number:	111392
Built:	1901 Chepstow
Builder:	Wm Hird
Owner:	H G Bryant, Bridgwater
Port of Registry:	Bridgwater
Net Reg Tons:	44
Dimensions:	74.6 x 17.1 x 5.7

A Severn trow originally open. Later, half boxed. Motorised 1927.

EFFORT

Official number:	17892
Buit:	1856 Stroud
Owners:	A Field, Saul
	A J Smith, Bristol
Port of Registry:	Gloucester
Net Reg Tons:	49
Dimensions:	74.7 x 18.5 x 9.0

A Severn trow still used as a floating workshop in 1950's at Worcester.

EFFORT

Official number:	81757
Built:	1880 Kingsbridge
Builder:	W Date
Owner:	Henry Grant, Kingsbridge
Port of Registry:	Salcombe
Net Reg Tons:	66
Dimensions:	67.7 x 18.6 x 8.2

Was in the sand trade from Torquay to Dartmouth and was tiller steered up to the 1930's.

EGREMONT

Official number:	85957
Built:	1892 Stonehouse, Plymouth
Builders:	Hawkes Brothers
Owner:	T Holman, Topsham
Signal Letters:	M.R.T.P.
Port of Registry:	Exeter
Net Reg Tons:	87
Dimensions:	87.2 x 21.6 x 9.6
Draught:	10.6

ELEANOR MARY

Official number:	44980
Built:	1865 Milford
Owners:	Saunders, Ilfracombe
	E J Peddar, Lynmouth
Port of Registry:	Bideford
Net Reg Tons:	44

First rigged as a schooner.

ELECTRIC

Official number:	62980
Built:	1871 Barnstaple
Builder:	William Westacott
Owner:	J Stoate, Watchet
Port of Registry:	Bridgwater
Net Reg Tons:	46
Dimensions:	63.8 x 19.6 x 7.9

First rigged as a smack. Wrecked Watchet 1903.

ELIZA

Official number:	56581
Built:	1865 Runcorn
Owners:	H Baker, Bridgwater
	G Reynolds, Berkeley
	T Eveleigh, Bridgwater
Port of Registry:	Bridgwater
Net Reg Tons:	54

A Severn trow. Survived as a barge until the 1930's.

ELIZA

Official number:	51203
Built:	1864 Bristol
Owners:	J Gollop, Lydney
	Mrs A Davis, Tidenham
Port of Registry:	Gloucester
Net Reg Tons:	57

A Severn trow. Broken up in 1940's.

ELIZA AND ANN

Official number:	1923
Built:	1845 Ilfracombe
Builder:	George Challacombe
Owner:	J Lemon, Appledore
Signal Letters:	H.M.B.F.
Net Reg Tons:	54
Port of Registry:	Bideford

Successively rigged as a smack then a schooner and finally as a ketch.

ELIZA ANNE

Official number:	69853
Built:	1877 Quayback, Cardigan
Owners:	John Evans, St Dogmells, Pembroke
	G Clarke, Braunton
Port of Registry:	Cardigan
Net Reg Tons:	32

ELIZA JANE

Official number:	67226
Built:	1873 Bridgwater
Builder:	G Gough
Owners:	J G Sully, Bridgwater
	Mrs M E Macarthy, Youghal
Signal Letters:	M.G.N.G.
Ports of Registry:	Bristol
	Bridgwater
Net Reg Tons:	98
Dimensions:	89.5 x 22.6 x 10.1

ELIZA MURRAY

Official number:	8689
Built:	1846 Arklow
Owners:	M Murray, Arklow
	P K Harris, Appledore
	Mrs Trick, Appledore
Port of Registry:	Bideford
Net Reg Tons:	39

ELIZABETH

Official number:	10886
Built:	1854 Bridgwater
Owners:	R S Roberts, Newport, Mon.
	J Bryant, Bridgwater
Signal Letters:	K.Q.H.R.
Port of Registry:	Bridgwater
Net Reg Tons:	36

ELIZABETH

Official number:	3864
Built:	1850
Owners:	G Hyatt, Lydney
	J Richardson, Chepstow
Port of Registry:	Bristol
Net Reg Tons:	49

A Severn trow.

Elizabeth. Wrecked Summerleaze Point, Bude, February 1912

ELIZABETH

Official number:	15324
Built:	1838 Appledore
Builder:	Thomas Evans
Owner:	Edward Edwards, Newport
Port of Registry:	Newport
Net Reg Tons:	29

ELIZABETH

Built:	1875 Appledore
Builder:	Thomas Green
Net Reg Tons:	60

First rigged as a polacca schooner. Later rerigged as a ketch.

ELIZABETH

Official number:	4458
Built:	1838 Salcombe
Owners:	John H Banbury, Bude
	W Drake, Braunton
Signal Letters:	J.C.P.F.
Port of Registry:	Bideford
Net Reg Tons:	51

Wrecked Bude 1912 whilst carrying coal from Newport.

ELIZABETH ANNE

Official number:	10913
Built:	1853 Polruan
Builder:	N & J Britson
Owners:	I Clarke, Minehead
	G Irwin, Combe Martin
Signal Letters:	K.Q.L.M.
Port of Registry:	Bridgwater
Net Reg Tons:	38
Dimensions:	49.3 x 15.3 x 7.2

Lengthened Appledore 1866.

ELIZABETH COUCH

Official number:	75408
Built:	1876 Ramsgate
Owners:	G M Goodman, Ramsgate
	James Watts, Braunton
Port of Registry:	Bideford
Net Reg Tons:	29

ELIZABETH SCOWN

Official number:	15592
Built:	1857 Bude
Builder:	R Stapleton
Owner:	O Davey, Bude
Signal Letters:	L.S.W.J.
Port of Registry:	Bideford
Net Reg Tons:	61

Wrecked off Bude.

ELSIE

Official number:	104758
Built:	1894 Galampton
Owners:	Henry L Summers, Ramsgate
	G Chugg, Braunton
Port of Registry:	Ramsgate
Net Reg Tons:	29

Broken up at The Pill, Braunton.

EMBLEM

Official number:	14046
Built:	1850 Padstow
Owners:	F Thomas, St Ives
	G Stoneman, Appledore
Signal Letters:	L.K.N.H.
Port of Registry:	Bideford
Net Reg Tons:	59

EMMA JANE

Official number:	29352
Built:	1861 Gunnel
Owners:	J Cowe, Padstow
	W B Williams, Newquay
Port of Registry:	Padstow
Net Reg Tons:	56
Dimensions:	71.1 x 19.1 x 8.6

First built as a schooner. Sunk in collision off Morte 1891.

EMILY

Official number:	102490
Built:	1895 Chepstow
Owners:	Lewis Aldridge, Arlingham
	Combwitch Farmers Association
Port of Registry:	Bristol
Net Reg Tons:	57

Foundered off Flatholm whilst taking coal to Bridgwater in 1934.

EMILY

Official number:	62906
Built:	1869 Jersey
Owners:	J Irwin, Chambercombe
	John Martin, Combe Martin
	and later in the Scilly Isles
Port of Registry:	Jersey
Net Reg Tons:	40

EMILY BARRATT

Official number:	125907
Built:	1913 Millom, Cumberland
Builder:	Gowon Shipbuilding Co
Owners:	G Welch, Braunton 1928-60
	P Herbert, Bude
	G Patterson 1984
Signal Letters:	J.V.B.P.
Port of Registry:	Barrow
Net Reg Tons:	51
Gross Reg Tons:	71
Dimensions:	76.8 x 20.0 x 8.3

One of the last two ketches built and the last wooden merchant sailing ship built in the U.K. believed to be the last ketch to have traded. Most of her life was spent in the trade to the Irish ports. Reported in 1983 after having been used for some years as a yacht to be going to Cumbria to be a sail training ship, after re-engining and repairs at Cooks Yard, Maldon. Winter 1983/4 having been salvaged after sinking whilst moored alongside at wharf near Tower Bridge in the Thames. July 1984 arrived Workington, Cumbria. Balloon barrage ship World War II at Falmouth.

Emily Barratt at Town Quay, Barnstaple, 1938

Figurehead of *Emily Barratt* at Maldon 1984

EMILY MARIA

Official number:	22967
Built:	1840 Castle Northwich
Owners:	H Burton, Newport
	A H Read, Liverpool
Port of Registry:	Newport
Net Reg Tons:	58

A Severn trow.

EMILY PRISCILLA

Official number:	99536
Built:	1894 Chepstow
Owner:	T Haling, Deerhurst
Port of Registry:	Gloucester
Net Reg Tons:	67

EMMA

Official number:	60581
Built:	1868 Bridgwater
Owners:	G Welch, Awre
	E Hamblin, Bridgwater
Port of Registry:	Bridgwater
Net Reg Tons:	47

A cutter rigged Severn trow.

EMMA

Official number:	15570
Built:	1845 Bideford
Owner:	Wm Drew, Bude
Port of Registry:	Bideford
Net Reg Tons:	49

Foundered in St Georges Channel.

EMMA LOUISE

Official number:	84475
Built:	1883 Barnstaple
Builder:	W Westacott
Owners:	S Berry, Barnstaple
	P S Rawle, Minehead
	J H Gorvin, Appledore
	H & F Drake, Braunton
	A Watts, Braunton
	P Herbert, Bude
Ports of Registry:	Aberdeen
	Barnstaple
Net Reg Tons:	66
Dimensions:	75.4 x 19.8 x 8.3

Emma Louise

Preserved in the North Devon Maritime Museum is her very ornamental figurehead complete with a painted Union Jack and elaborate scrollwork. Was the last wooden vessel built by Westacott. Originally a topsail schooner later converted to ketch rig. Was on the Lydney and Minehead coal trade and also traded to Ireland. Carried her last cargo in 1953. Her timbers lie on the banks of the River Torridge. Was the last trading vessel owned at Minehead. Engine fitted 1926.

EMPIRE

Official number:	22866
Built:	1854 United States
Owners:	T Doolittle, Wicklow
	Thomas H Fishwick, Appledore
Ports of Registry:	Barnstaple
	Liverpool
Net Reg Tons:	60

Originally schooner rigged and later converted to ketch rig. Stranded on Flatholm in 1886 but salvaged. In coal and gravel trade until lost in 1913.

EMPORER

Official number:	11727
Built:	1906 Chepstow
Owner:	T A Egelstaff, Bristol
Port of Registry:	Bristol
Net Reg Tons:	79
Length:	84'

A half boxed Severn trow. Was in the Lydney to Bristol coal trade.

EMU

Official number:	62045
Built:	1879 Truro
Owners:	T P Mitchell, Penryn
	J Knight, Lydney
Port of Registry:	Bideford
Signal Letters:	M.J.V.H.
Net Reg Tons:	50

Emporer. Trow originally ketch rigged at Bristol 1951

ENDEAVOUR

Official number:	15550
Built:	1822 Blyth
Owner:	T Symons, Bude
Port of Registry:	Bideford
Net Reg Tons:	45

A Severn trow. Wrecked off Bude.

ENERGY

Official number:	99540
Built:	1895 Saul
Owner:	William Sims, Saul, Gloucester
Port of Registry:	Gloucester
Net Reg Tons:	75

ENID

Official number:	108435
Built:	1898 Milford
Builder:	J W Francis
Owners:	Daniel Morgan, Aberayron, Cardigan
	W Chichester, Braunton
	Roland Chichester, Georgeham
	Mrs Chichester, N Devon
Port of Registry:	Barnstaple
Net Reg Tons:	30
Gross Tons:	44
Dimensions:	61.4 x 18.1 x 7.1
Draught:	7.11

Built of teak and loaded 68 tons of cargo. Fitted with 30 h.p. hot bulb diesel. Traded between S Wales and N. Devon ports in sand, coal and basic slag trade. Had an open wheel and reputed to be the only ketch Bermudan rigged. September 1939 was severely damaged when a heavy sea caused mainsheet to rip up pump and decking. The 6′ 3″ hole in the deck was covered with canvas and she was able to reach Ilfracombe. Reported sold abroad after World War II and left on a world cruise August 1951. Believed to have reached the West Indies.

EPNEY LASS

Official number:	27875
Built:	1860 Saul
Owner:	F Silbey, Epney, Gloucester
Signal Letters:	P.T.D.H.
Port of Registry:	Gloucester
Net Reg Tons:	64

ESCORT

Owner:	P L Hancort
Port of Registry:	Milford Haven
Net Reg Tons:	40

Sunk in collision off Lundy 1899.

EXCELSIOR

Official number:	93400
Built:	1891 Brimscombe
Owner:	Miss E Richardson, Chepstow
Port of Registry:	Gloucester
Net Reg Tons:	36

A Severn trow. Hulked at Purton 1951.

EXCELSIOR

Official number:	87607
Built:	1884 Gloucester
Owner:	F Hipwood, Gloucester
Port of Registry:	Gloucester
Net Reg Tons:	61

EXPRESS

Official number:	27880
Built:	1861 Swansea
Builder:	Wm Meager & son
Owners:	Mrs S Norman, Watchet
	William Stoate, Watchet
Signal Letters:	P.T.D.N.
Port of Registry:	Bridgwater
Net Reg Tons:	40
Dimensions:	58.7 x 18.2 x 7.9

Lost on Bideford Bar 1873.

FAIR FANNY

Official number:	92961
Built:	1886 Bideford
Builder:	H M Restarick
Owners:	Hewett & Co., Shadwell, London
Port of Registry:	
Net Reg Tons:	59

FAITH

Official number:	95133
Built:	1889 Plymouth
Owner:	Tregaskes, Bude
Port of Registry:	Plymouth
Net Reg Tons:	52

Lost Godrevy 1890.

FALCON

Official number:	26851
Built:	1858 Tarleton, Lancs
Owners:	C Darley, Blackburn
	W Morgan, Cardiff
	Clarke, Braunton
Port of Registry:	Cardiff
Net Reg Tons:	54

F.A.M.E. and *Kitty Ann*.
Blown ashore by gale at
Bow Weir,

l
F.A.M.E.
Official number:	81044
Built:	1880 Plymouth
Builder:	Hill
Owners;	B Tucker, Braunton, Stribling, Braunton
Signal Letters:	V.L.K.F.
Port of Registry:	Barnstaple
Net Reg Tons:	45
Dimensions:	56.3 x 17.9 x 7.8
Draught:	8.8

Lost after dismasting off Morte Stone, N Devon. Whilst on passage from Barnstaple to Ilfracombe with gravel May 1929 the mainmast was lost and the deck ripped up in heavy weather. The two crew were rescued by the ketch *Lewisman*.

FAME
Official number:	56361
Built:	1867 Bridgwater
Builder:	J Cough
Owner:	J C Hunt, Bridgwater
Signal Letters:	P.Q.M.W.
Port of Registry:	Bridgwater
Net Reg Tons:	61
Dimensions:	70.8 x 17.7 x 7.2

Stranded in 1915 but salvaged Western Bay. A square sailed Severn trow.

FAME
Official number:	14800
Built:	1841 Ironbridge
Owner:	F Hipwood, Gloucester
Port of Registry:	Gloucester
Net Reg Tons:	38

A Severn trow.

FANNY
Built:	1820 Barnstaple
Builder:	Chappel & Lovering
Owner:	Kemp, Braunton
Port of Registry:	Barnstaple
Net Reg Tons:	42
Dimensions:	46.6 x 14.2 x 8.

FANNY
Official number:	15564
Built:	1840 Bideford
Builder:	George Bragington
Owners:	J Kemp, Barnstaple
	W Tamplyn, Barnstaple
Signal Letters:	L.T.S.M.
Port of Registry:	Barnstaple
Net Reg Tons:	49

Lengthened 1843. First rigged as a sloop, then schooner and later ketch rigged.

FANNY
Official number:	68283
Built:	1872 Feock
Builder:	Scoble
Owners:	W Sarah, Plymouth
	J Ellis, Plymouth
	W D Crooks, Plymouth
	R S Hitchins, Truro
	W Slade, Appledore 1898–1907
Port of Registry:	Plymouth
Net Reg Tons:	53
Dimensions:	62 x 17 x 17.1

Lost on Lizard Rocks 1907, on passage Cadgwith to Lydney in ballast.

FANNY JANE

Official number:	10941
Built:	1858 Bridgwater
Builder:	Gough
Owners:	C J Symonds, Bridgwater
	B B Tazewell, Bridgwater
	Capt Westlake, Bridgwater
Signal Letters:	K.Q.N.H.
Port of Registry:	Bridgwater
Net Reg Tons:	61
Dimensions:	77.1 x 18.2 x 6.9

In her early days was in the Irish brick trade. Became a lighter 1958 and was still afloat in 1960. Was the last vessel to sail from Bridgwater without power.

FINIS

Official number:	78707
Built:	1881 Brimscombe
Owner:	F Wood, Westbury on Severn
Port of Registry:	Gloucester
Net Reg Tons:	27

A Severn trow. Carried stone from Chepstow to Tewkesbury and Osiers from Tewkesbury to Bristol. Ended her days as a breakwater at Arlington.

FISHGUARD LASS

Official number:	62792
Built:	1868 Milford
Owners:	W Prytharch, Llangian
	G Chugg, Braunton
Ports of Registry:	Padstow
	Barnstaple
Net Reg Tons:	34

In 1894 George Chugg aged 14 brought the vessel from Padstow to Ilfracombe on his own after his father had his leg broken by a falling gaff. Broken up at Vellator.

FLORENCE

Official number:	62739
Built:	1869 Saul
Owner:	R C Ring, Bristol
Port of Registry:	Bristol
Net Reg Tons:	61

A Severn trow.

FLORETTE (Formerly *The Moto* ketch)

Official number:	127083
Built:	1910 Millwall
Owners:	T Jones, Flint & B A Baker, Bristol
Signal Letters:	M.L.B.F.
Port of Registry:	Chester
Net Reg Tons:	82
Gross Tons:	109
Dimensions:	78 x 2.0.2 x 9

Sold after World War II to Brittany as a seaweed dredger.

Florrie

FLORRIE

Official number:	79360
Built:	1888 Appledore
Builder:	Robert Cock
Port of Registry:	Bideford
Net Reg Tons:	46

Was in the Newfoundland trade. Finished her days as a missionary vessel in the West Indies.

FLORRIE

Official number:	81533
Built:	1892 Bridgwater
Owner:	C J Symonds, Bridgwater
Signal Letters:	M.P.J.V.
Port of Registry:	Bridgwater
Net Reg Tons:	78
Dimensions:	81.8 x 21.1 x 8.8
Draught:	9.7

Sank off Milford Haven 1918 after stranding on Crowe Rock.

FOUR BROTHERS

Built:	Appledore
Owners:	F & E Corney, Braunton

Built as a schooner.

FLOWER O' PORTSOY

Official number:	69898
Built:	1875 Portsoy
Builder:	Smith
Owners:	J Paterson, Portsoy
	Arthur Galsworthy, Appledore
Signal Letters:	M.K.L.C.
Port of Registry:	Plymouth
Net Reg Tons:	70
Dimensions:	72.1 x 19.7 x 9.6
Draught:	10.7

On passage Cork for Appledore wrecked Balls Cove, Rosscarbery, Cork October, 1928 and broke up.

FLOWER OF THE SEVERN

Official number:	3897
Built:	1841 Lydney
Owners:	F H Poole, Bristol
	Wm Galbraith, Bristol
Signal Letters:	H.W.F.R.
Port of Registry:	Bristol
Net Reg Tons:	51

A Severn trow. Broken up in the 1940's.

FRANCES

Official number:	95902
Built:	1889 Falmouth
Builder:	Burt & Sons
Owner:	William Hutchings, Padstow
Signal Letters:	L.B.G.R.
Port of Registry:	Falmouth
	Padstow
Net Reg Tons:	72
Dimensions:	83.7 x 20.4 x 9.2
Draught:	10.1

Sunk by enemy action 1917.

FRANCIS BEDDOE

Official number:	70557
Built:	1877 Saundersfoot, Pembroke
Builder:	Read
Owners:	Mrs Betsy Beddoe, Appledore
	Phillip Harris, Appledore
Port of Registry:	Bideford
Net Reg Tons:	43
Dimensions:	60.4 x 17.6 x 7.8

Survived an exceptional gale in 1891 off the north Cornish coast whilst on passage to Bideford. Lost 1924. Was previously damaged in collision with steamer in River Avon in 1922.

Francis Beddoe at Appledore

FRIENDS

Official number:	16341
Built:	1844 Brockweir, Gloucestershire
Owner:	E T Silvey, Epney, Glos
Signal Letters:	M.B.D.K.
Port of Registry:	Gloucester
Net Reg Tons:	85

FRIENDS

Official number:	21552
Built:	1818 Appledore
Owners:	John Ridler, Minehead
	J Thoome, Watchet
Port of Registry:	Bridgwater
Net Reg Tons:	46

Lengthened 1853. Lost 1901 in Bristol Channel.

FRIENDSHIP

Official number:	11909
Built:	1857 Topsham
Owners:	A Stephens, Bude
	T Davey, Bude
Signal Letters:	K.V.N.T.
Port of Registry:	Bideford
Net Reg Tons:	59

Sank off Start Point 1908 whilst on passage St Malo to Tresco with slate.

FRIENDSHIP

Official number:	10896
Built:	1837 Watchet
Owners:	O Davey, Bude
	E Withers, Bridgwater
Port of Registry:	Bridgwater
Net Reg Tons:	54

GANNET

Official number:	10930
Built:	1825 Neath
Owners:	T Jenkins, Watchet
	E Saunders
	Hole, Watchet
Signal Letters:	K.Q.M.P.
Port of Registry:	Bridgwater
Net Reg Tons:	47
Dimensions:	41.4 x 15.2 x 5.0
Gross Tons:	70

GARABALDI

Official number:	47743
Built:	1864 Framilode, Glos
Owners:	J Knight, Gloucester
	W A Johns, Gloucester
Signal Letters:	V.T.P.R.
Port of Registry:	Gloucester
Net Reg Tons:	50

A Severn trow.

GARLANDSTONE

Official number:	128746
Built:	1909
Builder:	J Goss, Calstock
Owners:	Capt J J D Russam,
	Milford Haven 1909–19
	Capt A Murdoch, Gloucester 1919–41
	C M Couchman, Gloucester 1941–42
	L A Wingfield, London 1942–43
	R Parkhouse, Braunton 1943–58
	Capt Alf Parkhouse, Braunton 1943–58
	J Newcombe, Braunton 1943–58
	R A Kyffin & C Lansdown, Porthmadoc
Signal Letters:	M.K.X.V.
Port of Registry:	Milford
Net Reg Tons:	62
Gross Tons:	75.75
Dimensions:	76.0 x 20.2 x 9.0

Garlandstone ready for launching, 1909

Garlandstone – *continued*

Was principally in the trade with salt from Gloucester or coal from Lydney to south and west coast ports of Ireland. 2 Cyl paraffin engine fitted 40 b.h.p. 1912 and reengined 1949 75 b.h.p. one of the last two ketches built. During the Second World War was in the Irish trade owned by a Polish ship master. In the early 1970's went to Portmadoc for restoration and preservation and is now owned by the National Museum of Wales. In 1941 she was sailed singlehanded from S Ireland to Barry, S Wales. Was one of the last wooden sailing merchant vessels built in the U.K. and took 5 years to build.

GEM

Official number:	11938
Built:	1856 Ilfracombe
Builder:	Chas Dennis
Owner:	L Hart
Port of Registry:	Freetown S L
Net Reg Tons:	37

Lengthened 1863. Built as a schooner. Later dandy rigged and subsequently ketch rigged.

GEORGE

Official number:	11638
Built:	1839 Gloucetser
Owner:	A W White, Saul
Port of Registry:	Gloucester
Net Reg Tons:	64

Sank at mooring 1960. A Severn trow.

GEORGE

Official number:	63100
Built:	1873 Stonehouse
Owner:	G F Ford, Stonehouse
Port of Registry:	Gloucester

A Severn trow.

GEORGE MAY

Official number:	55629
Built:	1866 Guernsey
Owners:	J Vivian, Torquay
	Mrs S Norman, Watchet
Port of Registry:	Jersey
Net Reg Tons:	44
Gross Tons:	70

GEORGINA

Official number:	63080
Built:	1869 Saul
Owners:	A Williams, Bristol
	A Johns, Gloucester
Port of Registry:	Gloucester
Net Reg Tons:	52

A Severn trow.

GERTRUDE

Official number:	69912
Built:	1875 Saul
Owners:	S Butt, Stroud
	W Galbraith, Bristol
Port of Registry:	Gloucester
Net Reg Tons:	35

A Severn trow. Survived as a towing barge into the 1940's, bombed and broken up.

G H BEVAN

Official number:	60637
Built:	1869 Appledore
Owners:	J Rennie, Connahs Quay
	W H Marshall, West Looe, Cornwall
Signal Letters:	J.K.R.T.
Port of Registry:	Fowey
Net Reg Tons:	77

First rigged as a schooner.

GINEVRA

Official number:	17599
Built:	1857 Cowes
Owners:	J Masters, Swanage
	J Norman, Watchet
Signal Letters:	M.H.J.F.
Port of Registry:	Poole
Net Reg Tons:	41

GLOUCESTER PACKET

Official number:	11652
Built:	1824 Stroud
Builder:	F & J Oakes
Owners:	W Longley, Longley
	E Phillips Framilode
Signal Letters:	K.T.M.R.
Port of Registry:	Gloucester
Net Reg Tons:	59
Dimensions:	64.1 x 15.0 x 3.0

One of the early Severn trows.

GOLD SEEKER

Official number:	115011
Built:	1902 Rye
Owner:	E G Couter, Lowestoft
Port of Registry:	Lowestoft
Net Reg Tons:	62

GOOD HOPE

Official number:	3813
Built:	1847 Redbrook
Owner:	G Williams, Bristol
Signal Letters:	H.V.T.D.
Port of Registry:	Gloucester
Net Reg Tons:	58

A Severn trow.

GOOD HOPE

Official number:	4061
Built:	1840 Gloucester
Owners:	T Bennet, Saundersfoot
	J Beer, Newport
Signal Letters:	H.W.V.F.
Port of Registry:	Gloucester
Net Reg Tons:	28

GOOD TEMPLAR

Official number:	67835
Built:	1881 Goole
Owners:	G Sully, Bridgwater
	J L Hurman, Bridgwater
Signal Letters:	W.F.L.V.
Port of Registry:	Bridgwater
Net Reg Tons:	63

GOREY LASS

Official number:	55301
Built:	1868 Jersey
Owners:	Francis Stevens, Ilfracombe 1914–18
	Fred Harris, Appledore 1918–20
Port of Registry:	Jersey
Net Reg Tons:	44

First rigged as a dandy. Broken up Appledore 1920.

Good Intent

GOOD INTENT

Official number:	17131
Built:	1790 Plymouth
Owners:	G Dopen, Bridgwater
	J Woodland, Bridgwater
	Mrs M J Smart, Bridgwater
Port of Registry:	Bridgwater
Net Reg Tons:	25
Dimensions:	50.4 x 17.0

First rigged as a sloop. Taken by French privateer 1796.

GREENWOOD TREE

Official number:	92963
Built:	1886 Bideford
Builder:	H M Restarick
Owner:	H G Jones, Lowestoft
Port of Registry:	Lowestoft
Net Reg Tons:	64

HALCYON

Official number:	116167
Built:	1903 Hessle
Builder:	H Scarr
Owners:	Mark Aaron, Hull
	W McMillan, Hull
Signal Letters:	V.D.G.J.
Port of Registry:	Hull
Net Reg Tons:	91
Dimensions:	84.3 x 20.0 x 7.8

Broken up at Troon in the early 1970's

HALDON

Official number:	85958
Built:	1893 Stonehouse, Plymouth
Builder:	Hawke Bros
Owners:	Hook Shipping Co., Haverfordwest
	Slade, Appledore 1922-44
Signal Letters:	N. B. H. V.
Ports of Registry:	Exeter
	Kirkwall
	Barnstaple
Net Reg Tons:	96
Dimensions:	88 x 21.6 x 9.9

50 b.h.p. motor installed 1922. Converted to three-masted schooner 1924. Sold foreign in 1946 and was still trading as a motor ship in Icelandic waters in the 1950's.

HANNA (Ex *Margaretha*)

Official number:	144984
Built:	1915 Waterhuizen
Builder:	J J Patje & Zoom
Owners:	A Martell
	G Hartnoll, Braunton
	Capt Art Watts, Braunton
Port of Registry:	Poole
Net Reg Tons:	81
Gross Tons:	120
Dimensions:	91.3 x 21.1 x 7.9

Worked the small ports in the western end of the English Channel. Originally rigged as a two masted schooner. Wrecked at Etacq, Jersey on passage from Plymouth to Jersey with limestone 1949.

HANNAH

Official number:	63098
Built:	1872 Framilode
Owners:	R Hillman, Epney
	Mrs N H Nurse, Stonehouse
	T Burt, Padstow
Port of Registry:	Gloucester
Net Reg Tons:	58

One of the last of the flushed decked Severn trows rigged as an auxiliary ketch to trade carrying grain from Avonmouth to Gloucester until 1949.

HAPPY GO LUCKY

Oficial number:	3878
Built:	1841 Bridgnorth
Owners:	W Daw, Frampton on Severn
	D E Warren, Frampton on Severn
Port of Registry:	Gloucester
Net Reg Tons:	49

A Severn trow.

Hanna at Bristol 1939

HAPPY RETURN

Official number:	10308
Built:	1836 Gloucester
Owners:	J G Lovell, Bristol
	A J Smith, Bristol
Port of Registry:	Bristol
Net Reg Tons:	38

A Severn trow.

HARRIET

Official number:	13317
Built:	1827 Bower Yard, Salop
Owners:	C Cam, Arlingham
	T R Brown, Bristol
Port of Registry:	Gloucester
Net Reg Tons:	63

A Severn trow.

HAVELOCK

Official number:	
Built:	1858 Bideford
Builder:	George Cox
Net Reg Tons:	94

HAWK

Official number:	28141
Built:	1860 Appledore
Builder:	Wm Clibbett
Owners:	J Hooper, Bude
	F Hockin, Bude
Signal Letters:	P. V. G. B.
Port of Registry:	Bideford
Net Reg Tons:	36

First rigged as a schooner. Wrecked Bude 1897 whilst carrying scrap iron from Bude to Newport.

HEATHER BELL

Official number:	62974
Built:	1869 Barnstaple
Builder:	Wm Westacott
Owners:	J Allen, Watchet
	W K Slade, Appledore 1895-1922
Ports of Registry:	Bridgwater
	Barnstaple
Net Reg Tons:	53
Dimensions:	72 x 9.5 x 8.8

Originally rigged as a schooner, converted to ketch rig 1893. Whilst in Coverack in 1922 broke adrift in a heavy gale and broke up.

HEATHERBELL

Official number:	63370
Built:	1873 Cardigan
Owners:	T Clarke, Braunton
Signal Letters:	K.R.S.D.
Port of Registry:	Bideford
Net Reg Tons:	45

Lost off Irish coast about 1916.

HEDLEY

Official number:	
Built:	1866 Gunnislake, River Tamar
Builder:	Emmanuel Crocker

Originally a smack. Ketch rigged 1879.

HELSTONE

Official number:	17107
Built:	1831 Fowey
Owners:	J Furneaux, Penryn
	J Watts, Braunton
Signal Letters:	M.F.H.L.
Port of Registry:	Barnstaple
Net Reg Tons:	67

First rigged as a schooner.

HEMATOPE

Official number:	9514
Built:	1845 Paspebriac, Canada
Owners:	Wm Hutchings, Appledore
	George Eastlake, Appledore
Signal Letters:	K.H.G.F.
Port of Registry:	Bideford
Net Reg Tons:	56

First rigged as a brigantine. Condemned after running ashore Appledore about 1914.

HENRIETTA

Official number:	58727
Built:	1868 Goole
Builder:	Pearson
Owners:	T Davies, Cardigan
	T W Crouch
Signal Letters:	H.D.J.T.
Port of Registry:	Goole
Net Reg Tons:	68
Dimensions:	71.8 x 19.9 x 9.6
Draught:	10.4

Lost November 1925 near Abersoch.

HENRY

Official number:	10827
Built:	1812 Millwall
Owners:	T E Hodgson, Bridgwater
	S Taylor, Bridgwater
Port of Registry:	Bridgwater
Net Reg Tons:	47

Lost off Bude 1880.

HERBERT (formerly *Marcel*)

Official number:	62201
Owners:	Mrs E Swan, Knottingley
	J Red, Porlock
	R Williams, Wells
Port of Registry:	Wells
Net Reg Tons:	38

HIGRE

Official number:	69914
Built:	1876 Gloucester
Owner:	F Hipwood, Gloucester
Port of Registry:	Gloucester
Net Reg Tons:	41

A Severn trow. Hulked at Purton 1951.

H F BOLT

Official number:	76713
Built:	1876 Bideford
Builder:	John Johnson
Owners:	Capt Bolt, Appledore
	Wm Fishwick, Appledore
Signal Letters:	W.V.C.K.
Port of Registry:	Bideford
Net Reg Tons:	51
Dimensions:	71.6 x 19.6 x 8.7

In her early days was in the saltfish trade from Newfoundland and nuts from N Spanish ports to U.K. After being badly damaged, broke up in 1945 at Appledore and her hulk lies on the shore. Was the last ketch to trade without an engine.

H F Bolt

H H WILTON

Official number:	54561
Built:	1867 Saul, Gloucester
Owners:	W Vincent, Bristol
	H Field, Saul
Port of Registry:	Gloucester
Net Reg Tons:	70

A Severn trow

HOBAH

Official number:	81154
Built:	1879 Trellew Creek, Falmouth
Builder:	T Gray
	P Quennault
Owners:	Lemuel Hyett, Lydney
	Charles Lamey, Appledore
Signal Letters:	J.N.F.R.
Port of Registry:	Falmouth
Net Reg Tons:	56
Dimensions:	78.6 x 19.9 x 9.0
Draught:	9.6

In November 1908 she sailed from Appledore for Bude with coal. Owing to continual bad weather it was two months before she could enter Bude to discharge. Was sailed by Capt William Lamey from 1908 to 1940. 30 b.h.p. engine fitted 1911. Traded between Lydney and Cornish ports and reputed to have carried granite blocks to the Mediterranean in her early days for harbour building. Was the last ketch to discharge cargo at Newquay in 1922 and the last to discharge on the beach in 1937 at Port Luney. Laid up in the Torridge in 1940 and eventually broke up. Her hulk lies on the shore.

HONOUR

Official number:	45275
Built:	1862 Jersey
Owners:	Robert Pickett, Ilfracombe
	Spry, Ilfracombe
	S Mitchell, Braunton
	Capt T Butler, Braunton
Port of Registry:	Jersey
Net Reg Tons:	31

HOPE

Official number:	97479
Built:	1891 Plymouth
Owner:	Thomas Roe, Looe
Port of Registry:	Plymouth
Net Reg Tons:	28

At one time rigged as a Polacca brig.

HOWARD

Official number:	82977
Built:	1884 Neyland
Owner:	N Tremayne, Maunan
Signal Letters:	J.G.W.L.
Port of Registry:	Milford
Net Reg Tons:	50

HUMILITY

Official number:	8421
Built:	1838 Littlehampton
Owners:	Welch & Co
	T Pow, Appledore
Signal Letters:	K.C.D.L.
Port of Registry:	Chichester
	Bideford
Net Reg Tons:	49

Was in trade until 1920.

Humility

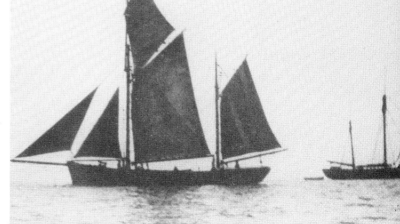

I'LL TRY

Official number:	1432
Built:	1853 Barnstaple
Builder:	Robert Johnson
Owner:	W Gafney, Wexford
Port of Registry:	Wexford
Net Reg Tons:	56

First rigged as a schooner. Went ashore Woolacombe 1859.

INDEPENDENT

Official number:	3926
Built:	1823 Brimscombe
Owners:	F H Poole, Bristol
	Wm Galbraith, Bristol
Port of Registry:	Bristol
Net Reg Tons:	54

A Severn trow.

INDUSTRY

Official number:	11610
Built:	1847 Cambridge, Glos
Owners:	R Gazard, Berkeley
	T Richardson, Chepstow
Signal Letters:	K.T.H.W.
Port of Registry:	Gloucester
Net Reg Tons:	19

A Severn trow.

INDUSTRY

Official number:	47965
Built:	1871 Chepstow
Owner:	W Jones, Lydney
Port of Registry:	Chepstow
Net Reg Tons:	29

A Severn trow.

INDUSTRY

Official number:	11657
Built:	1865 Stourport
Owner:	Mrs S Watkins
Signal Letters:	K.T.N.C.
Port of Registry:	Gloucester
Net Reg Tons:	56

A Severn trow.

INDUSTRY

Official number:	20981
Built:	1845 Bridgnorth
Owner:	W F Washbourne, Gloucester
Port of Registry:	Gloucester
Net Reg Tons:	52

A Severn trow.

INDUSTRY

Official number:	60677
Built:	1867 Gloucester
Builder:	J Davies
Owners:	W Holding, Bridgwater
	J Jones, Llanangan
Signal Letters:	Q.T.D.H.
Port of Registry:	Bridgwater
Net Reg Tons:	64
Dimensions:	79.0 x 18.6 x 9.1
Draught:	9.8

INVICTA (Ex Good & Blanchard)

Official number:	91545
Built:	1885 Hull
Owners:	J Hellyer, Hull
	J Jewell, Appledore
Signal Letters:	R.T.V.P.
Port of Registry:	Bideford
Net Reg Tons:	73

Irene at Bideford Shipyard

IRENE

Official number:	111394
Built:	1907 Bridgwater
Builder:	J F Carver & Son Ltd
Owners:	W Lee, Bridgwater
	C J Symons, Bridgwater
	S Symons, Bridgwater
	Dr L Morrish, 1965
Signal Letters:	H. K. V. S.
Port of Registry:	Bridgwater
Net Reg Tons:	77
Gross Tons:	98
Dimensions:	85.5 x 21.0 x 9.1
Draught:	9.9

Last sailing vessel built at Bridgwater. Originally traded to the continent and subsequently in the brick trade to Liverpool and Ireland. Was the last ketch in trade in U.K. waters and traded until 1960. Laid up at Appledore for a year and then moved to Hamble River. 40 h.p. invincible engine fitted 1919. Replaced by 70 h.p. Bolinder 1921, Ellwe Suenska 1939 and Gardner diesel 1979. Badly damaged by fire 1972. Dry docked for overhaul and underwater repairs at Gloucester 1982. Lay in the River Colne, Essex during the winter of 1982/3 where a new rudder and sails were fitted in 1984. Took part in the tall ships European race from Denmark to Greenock and was in the parade of sail in the Mersey. Now fitted with 135 h.p. diesel engine. Attended "Sail Amsterdam" gathering of tall ships 1985. Currently winters at Bristol and used for charter work.

Irene, Bideford 1985

Irene being launched Bridgwater 1907

IRON KING (Ex *Desmond*)

Official number:	91067
Built:	1864 Reputedly in India
Owners:	William A Acford, Appledore
	J Watts, Braunton
Port of Registry:	Bideford
Net Reg Tons:	43
Dimensions:	77.0 x 17.6 x 7.1
Draught:	7.11

Lengthened by 14' in 1891 by William Whitfield at Higher Cleave, Bideford and became 60 tons registered, being converted from a yacht. In collision off Lundy November 1922. Towed into Padstow. On the gravel trade to Bristol and coal from Lydney. Later renamed *Saltash*.

ISABEL

Official number:	79029
Built:	1878 Sunderland
Owners:	W M Acford, Appledore
	Thomas Brooks, Appledore
	T Watts, Braunton
	A Corney, Braunton
Signal Letters:	S.F.C.H.
Port of Registry:	Bideford
Net Reg Tons:	81

Set off on world cruise 1947.

ISABELLA

Official number:	62772
Built:	1872 Freckleton
Owners:	A L Jones, Gloucester
	R Orchard, Padstow
Signal Letters:	Q.D.N.H.
Port of Registry:	Gloucester
Net Reg Tons:	72

Originally schooner rigged, became a hulk, Cant Cove, River Camel and broke up in early 1960's.

J & A R

Official number:	99535
Built:	1894 Saul
Owner:	A S Rice, Gloucester
Port of Registry:	Gloucester
Net Reg Tons:	66

A Severn trow. Hulked at Purton 1951.

Remains of *Isabella* 1961

JMJ

Official number:	56030
Built:	1867 Bideford
Builder:	Thomas Waters
Owner:	W Hunt, Braunton
Signal Letters:	J.H.N.S.
Port of Registry:	Barnstaple
Net Reg Tons:	
Dimensions:	74.0 x 18.7 x 9.6

Lost after running ashore at Ailsa Craig 1910.

J W V

Official Number:	65522
Built:	1871 Restronguet
Builder:	J Stephens
Owners:	J H Vinton, Taibach, Glamorgan 1871-77
	W Slade & G Quance, Appledore 1903-09
Port of Registry:	Chester
Net Reg Tons:	58
Dimensions:	76.0 x 17.9 x 9.6

First rigged as a schooner. Run down Southampton Water 1909 whilst on passage to Newport with scrap iron and became a barge at Par.

JANE

Built:	1802 Bideford
Owners:	May & Co
	Thomas Burnard, Bideford
Port of Registry:	Padstow
Net Reg Tons:	64
Length:	53'

First rigged as a brigantine. Lost January 1868.

JANE

Official number:	18599
Built:	1851 Swansea
Owners:	John Irwin, Combe Martin
	George Irwin, Combe Martin
Port of Registry:	Barnstaple
Net Reg Tons:	31

First smack rigged later rerigged as a ketch.
Was lengthened twice.

JANE

Official number:	11641
Built:	1810 Bridgnorth
Owner:	W Davies, Saul
Signal Letters:	K.T.M.B.
Port of Registry:	Gloucester
Net Reg Tons:	66

JANE

Official number:	26713
Built:	1800 Runcorn
Owners:	Wm Smart, Bridgwater
	H J Winslade, Bridgwater
	Peter Hart, Uphill
Signal Letters:	P.G.M.T.
Port of Registry:	Bridgwater
Net Reg Tons:	37
Dimensions:	61.8 x 14.5 x 5.2

Sloop rigged when first built. Altered to ketch rig 1881 and registered tons increased to 40. Hulked in 1925 and used for coal storage. Sank at her mooring 1936. Broken up for firewood Lydney 1939 at which time she was the oldest British merchant vessel afloat. As a Bristol Channel trow in her earlier years she carried railway materials between Wales and the Severn ports.

JANE & ELIZABETH

Official number:	1064
Built:	1842 Appledore
Builder:	Thomas Green
Owner:	J Butler, Bickington
Signal Letters:	H.G.L.V.
Port of Registry:	Swansea
Net Reg Tons:	68

First rigged as a schooner later rerigged as a ketch.

JANE & SARAH

Official number:	16048
Built:	1855 Padstow
Builder:	E Trevetmam Bennett
Owners:	J Owens, Bangor
	Mrs H Ayre, Wrafton

Isabella and *Jane*, Padstow 1936

Signal Letters:	L.V.S.R.
Ports of Registry:	Padstow
	Barnstaple
Net Reg Tons:	44
Dimensions:	58.6 x 15.4 x 7.7

Broken up at the Pill, Braunton in the early 1930's.

JANETTE

Official number:	60329
Built:	1867 Glasgow
Owner:	N Doyle, Skerries, Dublin
Signal Letters:	J.R.M.Q.
Port of Registry:	Glasgow
Net Reg Tons:	68

Broken up 1922.

JESSAMINE

Official number:	76715
Built:	1878 Bude
Owners:	J T Hooper, Bude
	E Maynard, Bude
Signal Letters:	R.Q.K.M.
Port of Registry:	Bideford
Net Reg Tons:	59

Sold to Liverpool owners.

Jessie leaving Bude

JESSIE
Official number:	27266
Built:	1859 Port Glasgow
Owners:	R Wilson, St Andrews
	N H Tregaske, Bude
Signal Letters:	Q.L.H.R.
Port of Registry:	Bideford
Net Reg Tons:	43

J MILTON
Official number:	65317
Built:	1872 Saul, Gloucester
Builder:	F Evans
Owners:	J D Nurse, Bridgwater
	Wm Vincent, Bristol
	David Nurse, Bridgwater
	Herbert I Smith, Newport, Mon
	Grain Coasters Ltd, Newport, Mon
	B I Transport Co Ltd, London
	Joseph Rank Ltd, London
Port of Registry:	Bridgwater
Net Reg Tons:	91
Dimensions:	84.5 x 22.0 x 9.5

Broken up Barry Docks 1956.

JOE ABRAHAM
Official number:	15331
Built:	1850 Egremont Bay,
	Prince Edward Isle, Canada
Builder:	James Yeo
Owner:	T Cook
Port of Registry:	
Net Reg Tons:	36
Dimensions:	46.0 x 15.3 x 7.5

JOHANN CARL
Official number:	105153
Built:	1893 Seedorf
Builder:	G Kruger, Germany
Owners:	E Morgan, Cardigan
	Alex Stephens, Porth, Cornwall
Port of Registry:	Padstow
	Guernsey
Net Reg Tons:	45
Dimensions:	65.0 x 18.4 x 7.9

Built as a schooner. Ketch rigged early 1900's. Lost or sandbank Cleveden 1917.

JOHN & ANN
Official number:	15333
Built:	1840 Barnstaple
Builder:	John Westacott
Owners:	Chugg, Braunton
	H Drake, Wrafton
Siganl Letters:	L.R.V.K.
Port of Registry:	Barnstaple
Net Reg Tons:	38

Built as a smack. Later rerigged as a ketch.

JOHN & WILLIAM
Official number:	19133
Built:	1859 Porlock Weir
Builder:	William Pulsford
Owners:	D Haver, Taunton
	John Ridler, Minehead
	William Pulsford, Minehead
Signal Letters:	M.Q.R.K.
Port of Registry:	Bridgwater
Net Reg Tons:	36
Dimensions:	45.8 x 17.1 x 6.8

First rigged as a smack. Lost Barry 1894.

JOHNNY TOOLE
Official number:	92952
Built:	1886 Yarmouth
Owners:	Hewett & Co., Shadwell
	J C Coxon, Newport
Port of Registry:	Newport
Net Reg Tons:	62

JONADAH

Official number:	26731
Built:	1848 Newport
Owners:	J Miles, Bristol
	Mrs L James, Saul, Gloucester
Signal Letters:	P.M.J.B.
Port of Registry:	Bristol
Net Reg Tons:	68

A Severn trow rebuilt and decked in 1895. Became a motor barge 1948 and later a coal hulk.

JOSEPH & MARY

Official number:	22096
Built:	1839 Llandogo
Owners:	W Davis, Tiddenham
	Mrs E Rowles, Frampton on Severn
Port of Registry:	Chepstow
Net Reg Tons:	25

A Severn trow.

JOSEPH & THOMAS

Official number:	5688
Built:	1834 Fowey
Rebuilt:	1889
Owner:	B Shazel, Bude
Signal Letters:	J.K.R.D.
Ports of Registry:	Bideford
	Bude
Net Reg Tons:	38

Lost 1888 off Bude.

JULIA

Official number:	75261
Built:	1876 Bideford
Builder:	John Johnson
Owners:	A MacMahon, Newport
	B Lamey, Appledore
Signal Letters:	K.P.W.N.
Port of Registry:	Bideford
Net Reg Tons:	58

JULIA

Official number:	47304
Built:	1863 Milton, Kent
Owners:	R H Dulton, Romsey
	T R Brown, Bristol
Port of Registry:	Bristol
Net Reg Tons:	69

Julia at Bideford Quay

JULIE

Official number:	84514
Built:	1889 Malpas
Owners:	Nobels Explosive Co., Glasgow
	J Chichester, Braunton
Port of Registry:	Barnstaple
Net Reg Tons:	38

KATE

Official number:	78472
Built:	1877 Hakin, Milford
Owners:	J L Davies, Milford
	W J Canton, Pembroke
	Capt Jones, Braunton
Port of Registry:	Milford
Net Reg Tons:	26

KATE

Official number:	45357
Built:	1863 Waterford
Owner:	W J Greenaway, Saul, Gloucester
Signal Letters:	V.C.W.G.
Port of Registry:	Gloucester
Net Reg Tons:	64

KATIE & ANNIE

Official number:	99537
Built:	1894 Bridgwater
Owner:	T Stamp, Stonehouse
Port of Registry:	Gloucester
Net Reg Tons:	79

KETCH

Official number:	99732
Built:	1894 Fairlie
Builder:	W Fife & Son
Owners:	A F Sutherland, Thurso
	J Jewell, Appledore
Port of Registry:	Bideford
Net Reg Tons:	56
Dimensions:	69.0 x 19.7 x 8.5
Draught:	9.2

Balloon barrage defence ship 1939–45.
Her hulk lies on the bank of the River Torridge

KINGS OAK

Official number:	89060
Built:	1884 Southtown
Builder:	H Fellows & Son
Owner:	R Harris, Watchet
Port of Registry:	Cardiff
Net Reg Tons:	58
Gross Tons:	100
Dimensions:	82.2 x 19.5 x 9.4
Draught:	10.0

First rigged as a dandy. In January 1923 lost gear in heavy weather. Went into Swansea and did not rise to tide. Became submerged but later refloated and repaired. Broken up Appledore later that year.

KINDLY LIGHT

Official number:	105242
Built:	1896 Falmouth
Builder:	Burt
Owner:	J B Cooke, Bude
Signal Letters:	P.G.D.S.
Port of Registry:	Bideford
Net Reg Tons:	90
Dimensions:	85.1 x 21.8 x 9.4
Draught:	9.10

An iron ketch sunk off Bude by submarine during World War I.

KITTY ANN

Official number:	15349
Built:	1856 Appledore
Builder:	Thomas Green
Owner:	C Chugg, Braunton
Signal Letters:	L.R.W.F.
Port of Registry:	Barnstaple
Net Reg Tons:	49
Dimensions:	61.0 x 18.1 x 8.5

Kitty Ann

Built as a brigantine later schooner rigged and subsequently as a ketch. Was in the Irish trade and one of the first ketches to have an engine fitted. Broken up at Braunton in the early 1930's.

LADY AGNES

Official number:	68865
Built:	1877 St Agnes
Owners:	N F Hutchings, St Agnes
	J Williams, Portmadoc
	R Jones, Aberystwyth
	C Couch
Signal Letters:	H.N.G.B.
Port of Registry:	Aberystwyth
Net Reg Tons:	70

Originally schooner rigged and in china clay trade.

LADY OF THE ISLES

Official number:	55302
Built:	1868 Jersey
Owners:	J Watts, Braunton
	J Davies, Saundersfoot
	H Irwin, Combe Martin
Signal Letters:	K.C.D.Q.
Port of Registry:	Milford
Net Reg Tons:	36

First rigged as a dandy.

Lavinia

LADY OF THE LAKE

Official number:	68590
Built:	1876 Bosham
Builder:	T Smart
Owners:	T Smart, Bosham 1876–1910
	Mrs S Quance, Appledore 1910–1916
Signal Letters:	W.V.M.C.
Port of Registry:	Portsmouth
Net Reg Tons:	79
Dimensions:	78.1 x 19.6 x 9.6

Sunk by submarine U17, 1916 off Start Point whilst on passage to Treport with coal. Crew taken prisoner. Released into ship's boat after 24 hours and rescued by naval patrol.

LADY OF THE LAKE

Official number:	29842
Built:	1862 Bideford
Builder:	Sloman
Owners:	J Hooper, Bude
	D Stevens, Bude
Signal Letters:	Q.H.J.L.
Port of Registry:	Bideford
Net Reg Tons:	51

First rigged as a schooner. Wrecked on Bude sands 1898 while carrying coal from Newport to Bude.

LARK

Official number:	10937
Built:	1856 Bridgwater
Owners:	O Davies, Maentwrog Merioneth
	T Bassett, Braunton
	J Chichester, Braunton
Signal Letters:	K.Q.N.C.
Port of Registry:	Cardiff
Net Reg Tons:	36

Carried ammunition for the Government before World War I.

LAVINIA

Official number:	62754
Built:	1870 Ardossan
Builder:	P Barclay & Son
Owner:	J Wetherspoon, Clackaig, Argyll
Ports of Registry:	Irvine
	Bridgwater
Net Reg Tons:	51
Dimensions:	69.1 x 18.8 x 7.8

First rigged as a schooner. Wrecked Wexford 1915.

LEADER

Official number:	91389
Built:	1884 Hull
Builder:	G W Ewing & Co
Owners:	T Scilly, Appledore
	T Burt, Gloucester
Signal Letters:	Q.F.H.K.
Port of Registry:	Bideford
Net Reg Tons:	65
Dimensions:	79.7 x 20.0 x 10.1
Draught:	11.2

Built as an iron trawler and converted to cargo carrying. Sank after hitting submerged rock Flimstone Head December 1928.

LENORA

Official number:	19225
Built:	1854 Padstow
Builder:	E Trevetman Bennett
Owners:	Mrs E Heal, Fremington
	Mrs M J Chichester, Braunton
Signal Letters:	M.R.C.P.
Ports of Registry:	Padstow
	Barnstaple
Net Reg Tons:	29
Dimensions:	52.8 x 15.3 x 7.3

First built as a smack and converted to a ketch in the 1880's.

LEWISMAN

Official number:	79131
Built:	1878 Stornway
Owners:	W Sarah, Plymouth 1884–95
	W Holden 1895–1901
	W Slade, Appledore 1901–27
	S W Slatter, Barnstaple 1927–1946
	Mitchell, Braunton
Ports of Registry:	Bideford
	Leith
Net Reg Tons:	58
Dimensions:	90.1 x 18.1 x 8.1

First rigged as a schooner. Converted to ketch 1889. Engine fitted in 1927. Sold to Scottish owners after World War II. Broken up at Granton about 1949.

Lewisman at Barnstaple 1938

56

LIBERTY

Official number:	13843
Built:	1838 Ilfracombe
Owners:	W Bate, Padstow
	J Watts, Braunton
Signal Letters:	L.J.Q.T.
Port of Registry:	Padstow
Net Reg Tons:	52

Built as a smack converted to schooner and later ketch rigged. Sold as a hulk at Swansea 1905.

LILLEA VENN

Official number:	28502
Built:	1860 Bristol
Owner:	Severn & Canal Carrying Co, Gloucester
Port of Registry:	Bristol
Net Reg Tons:	57

A Severn trow.

LILY

Official number:	108020
Built:	1897 Penryn
Owners:	P H Dawe, Penzance
	E D Anderton, Falmouth
	D Kingsland, Topsham
	A Oxenham, Lynmouth 1916–1928
	H F Stevens, Tonbridge
	F J Bennet, Ilfracombe
	Clevedon & Portishead
	Light Railway Co 1929
Port of Registry:	Bideford
Net Reg Tons:	25
Dimensions:	56.0 x 16.0 x 5.7

Motor fitted 1927. Foundered off River Usk 1929. The last trading vessel owned from Lynmouth.

LINDA

Official number:	78190
Built:	1878 Falmouth
Builder:	Burt
Owners:	N Gray, Penryn
	F Drake, Braunton
Signal Letters:	S.N.G.T.
Port of Registry:	Barnstaple
Net Reg Tons:	34
Dimensions:	57.3 x 17.1 x 7.6
Draught:	8.2

Lost in collision 1900.

LITTLE JANE

Official number:	19761
Built:	1858 Newquay
Owners:	J William, Oreston
	J Crocombe, Lynmouth
	Norman, Watchet
Signal Letters:	M.T.H.J.
Port of Registry:	Plymouth
Net Reg Tons:	47
Gross Tons:	70

Lost Clovelly 1910.

LIVELY

Official number:	22536
Built:	1859 Cowes
Owners:	N H Copp, Exmouth
	W H Hobbs, Appledore
Signal Letters:	N.L.V.H.
Port of Registry:	Bideford
Net Reg Tons:	54
Length:	72

Originally smack rigged and reputed to have been a pilot cutter in her early days. Lengthened and ketch rigged in 1867, In coal and gravel trade between Appledore and Avonmouth and also to Boscastle and was the last ketch to trade there up to World War I. Lost 1922.

LIZZIE

Official number:	67956
Built:	1873 Stromness
Builder:	G & P Copland
Owners:	A Nicholas, Watchet
	Chidgey, Watchet
Port of Registry:	Bridgwater
Net Reg Tons:	66
Gross Tons:	100
Dimensions:	68.1 x 20.1 x 8.9

LONGNEY LASS

Official number:	11611
Built:	1842 Bridgnorth
Owners:	T Hobbs, Frampton on Severn
	W W Long, Saul
Port of Registry:	Gloucester
Net Reg Tons:	60

A Severn trow.

LUCIE OF DUNDALK

Official number:	76254
Built:	1881 Dundalk
Owners:	C D King, Annagasson
	Welch, Braunton
Port of Registry:	Dundalk
Net Reg Tons:	52

Balloon barrage ship at Falmouth during Second World War.

LOOE

Official number:	10815
Built:	1787 Looe
Owners:	J Taylor, Bridgwater
	W Walter, Ilfracombe
	T K Ridler
Signal Letters:	K.Q.B.W.
Port of Registry:	Bridgwater
Net Reg Tons:	38
Dimensions:	53.7 x 18.6 x 7.7

Smack rigged to 1870 when ketch rigged. In commission until 1905 when broken up at Minehead.

LOUISA

Official number:	28950
Built:	1860 Dartmouth
Owner:	T Chidgey, Watchet
Signal Letters:	Q.C.N.U.
Port of Registry:	Dartmouth
Net Reg Tons:	62

LOUISE

Official number:	6949
Built:	1877 Newquay
Builder:	Chegwidden
Owner:	T Chidgey, Watchet
Signal Letters:	Q.N.J.V.
Port of Registry:	Padstow
Net Reg Tons:	93
Gross Tons:	100
Dimensions:	87.4 x 22.9 x 11.0
Draught:	11.6

First rigged as a schooner. Part of her hull was used as a breakwater at Falmouth 1937.

LOVELY SUSAN

Official number:	3854
Built:	1839 Whitminster
Owners:	P Clutterbuck, Whitminster
	M & C Gower, Cardiff
Signal Letters:	H.W.B.T.
Port of Registry:	Gloucester
Net Reg Tons:	55

A Severn trow.

LUCY

Official number:	62899
Built:	1871 Bideford
Owners:	J Cruse, Clovelly
	J T Moss, Clovelly
Port of Registry:	Bideford
Net Reg Tons:	25

LYDNEY PACKET

Official number:	11721
Built:	1849 Lydney
Owners:	P Grimes, Lydney
	Mrs E Cook, Saul
Port of Registry:	Gloucester
Net Reg Tons:	43

A Severn trow.

MABEL

Official number:	68789
Built:	1875 Jersey
Builder:	Allix
Owners:	H Shepherd, Cardiff
	W J Land, Appledore
Signal Letters:	K.M.H.D.
Port of Registry:	Bideford
Net Reg Tons:	60
Dimensions:	75.9 x 19.6 x 9.2

First rigged as a schooner.

MAGGIE ANNIE

Official number:	78706
Built:	1881 Bridgwater
Builder:	F J Carver
Owners:	A Corney, Braunton
	W Drake, Braunton
Signal Letters:	W.G.F.V.
Port of Registry:	Barnstaple
Net Reg Tons:	59
Dimensions:	76.5 x 20.2 x 9.0

MARGARET

Official number:	63079
Built:	1869 Gloucester
Owner:	J Stamp, Par
Port of Registry:	Gloucester
Net Reg Tons:	73

MARGARET

Official number:	105244
Built:	1903 Plymouth
Builder:	W Shilston
Owner:	J Lamey, Appledore
Port of Registry:	Bideford
Net Reg Tons:	42
Dimensions:	68.8 x 18.4 x 7.0

MARGARET DAVIES

Official number:	44247
Built:	1863 Maesygarnedd
Owners:	W Morris, Barmouth
	S E Ford, Appledore
Signal Letters:	T.S.H.Q.
Port of Registry:	Caernarvon
Net Reg Tons:	48

MARJORIE

Official number:	112466
Built:	1904 Castlepill
Builder:	J W Francis
Owner:	William Drake, Braunton
Port of Registry:	Barnstaple
Net Reg Tons:	74

MARIAN

Official number:	56370
Built:	1869 Bridgwater
Builder:	J Gough
Owner:	T Rowles, Bridgwater
Port of Registry:	Bridgwater
Net Reg Tons:	59

MARS

Official number:	10324
Built:	1856 Chalford
Owner:	J Chapman, Chalford
Port of Registry:	Bristol
Net Reg Tons:	23

A Severn trow.

MARS

Built:	1819 Bideford
Builder:	John Crocker
Net Reg Tons:	48
Dimensions:	48.1 x 15.2 x 8.6

Did at least two Atlantic crossings.

MARTIN LUTHER

Official number:	19671
Built:	1847 Cowes
Owners:	W Woodnutt, Newport, IOW
	L Smart, Uphill
	F Pemberthy, Weston Super Mare
Signal Letters:	M.S.W.H.
Port of Registry:	Cowes
Net Reg Tons:	34

Martin Luther in river Parret, Bridgwater

MARY
Official number:	14369
Built:	1856 Bristol
Owner:	Severn & Canal Carrying Co
Port of Registry:	Bristol
Net Reg Tons:	51

A Severn trow.

MARY
Official number:	18967
Built:	
Owners:	J Gough, Bridgwater
	W T Gibbs, Bridgwater
	E J Pedder, Lynmouth
Port of Registry:	Bridgwater
Net Reg Tons:	26

In Lynmouth Capt J Chichester was ordered by the owner to sail on a Sunday. He refused for religious reasons packed his bag, was given his discharge papers and left the ship.

MARY
Official number:	11341
Built:	1819 Ironbridge, Salop
Owner:	E Davis, Saul
Port of Registry:	Bristol
Net Reg Tons:	54

MARY
Official number:	127411
Built:	1907 Pembroke
Owners:	G P Francis, Pembroke Dock
	Scobling, Braunton
Port of Registry:	Milford
Net Reg Tons:	84

Broken up Braunton Pill in early 1930's.

MARY
Official number:	63097
Built:	1872 Brimscombe, Gloucester
Owner:	G T Beard, Gloucester
Port of Registry:	Gloucester
Net Reg Tons:	50

A Severn trow.

MARY ANN
Official number:	63082
Built:	1870 Gloucester
Owner:	W Butler, Bristol
Port of Registry:	Gloucester
Net Reg Tons:	38

MARY ANN
Official number:	62733
Built:	1868 Bristol
Owner:	R Engelstaff, Bristol
Port of Registry:	Bristol
Net Reg Tons:	31

A Severn trow.

MARY ANN
Official number:	13319
Built:	1827 Stourport
Owner:	W Cook, Frampton on Severn
Signal Letters:	L.G.M.V.
Port of Registry:	Gloucester
Net Reg Tons:	43

MARY ELIEZER
Official number:	118818
Built:	1904 Hammilwarder, Germany
Builder:	C Luhring
Owners:	James Gladhill, Barton on Humber
	G Clarke, Braunton
Signal Letters:	H.B.M.Q.
Port of Registry:	Hull
Net Reg Tons:	66
Dimensions:	81.6 x 18.0 x 7.7

Mary Eliezer in the Exeter Canal

MARY SEYMOUR

Official number:	47040
Built:	1865 Padstow
Builder:	Tredwen
Owners:	J Hawke, Port Isaac
	B Harvey, Padstow
Signal Letters:	V.L.W.T.
Port of Registry:	Portsmouth
Net Reg Tons:	138
Dimensions:	97.0 x 23.2 x 11.6

First rigged as a schooner later rerigged as a ketch.

MARY ELIEZER – *continued*

Used to work the ports at the western end of the English Channel. In 1932 accidentally hit by practice torpedo in Portland. Survived by master plugging hole with a bag. Store ship to R.N. 1939-1945. Traded Bristol Channel in grain and slag from Swansea to Barnstaple and Bideford. Sold to Danish owners 1947. At some time was the stone fisher and named *Stenbideren*. Later sold to Dutch owners.

MARY GRACE

Official number:	15323
Built:	1852 Appledore
Builder:	Thomas Green
Owners:	William Corney, Wrafton
	Chugg, Braunton
	Clarke, Braunton
Port of Registry:	Barnstaple
Net Reg Tons:	31

Motor installed 1917.

MARY LOUISA (Formerly *St Pierre*)

Official number:	29216
Built:	1849 France
Owners:	H J Watts, Watchet
	J H Nicholas, Watchet
Signal Letters:	Q.D.R.P.
Port of Registry:	Bridgwater
Net Reg Tons:	61

MARY STEWART

Official number:	60618
Built:	1876 Montrose
Owners:	J Stewart, Strone, Argyll
	George Meadows, Stonehouse
	Capt W Parkhouse, Braunton 1925-58
	Peter Herbert, Bude
	J Cohen & R Waller, U S A
Port of Registry:	Greenock
Net Reg Tons:	59
Length:	72.0

First rigged as a two masted schooner built of steel. Converted to ketch rig 1903. In her early days was in Newfoundland trade and china clay trade from Fowey. One of the last ketches to have a figurehead which was lost in heavy weather in 1939. Also about the last ketch to carry a jiboom in addition to a bowsprit. Store ship for R N 1939-45. Engine fitted 1924. Sold to an American owner 1963 and delivered to Santander, Spain by Peter Herbert. Reported still at Santander about 1970.

Mary Stewart at Rolle Quay, Barnstaple 1938

Maude at Rolle Quay, Barnstaple 1939

MAUDE

Official number:	62010
Built:	1865 Widnes
Owners:	Thomas Knight, Lydney
	B Tucker, Braunton
	R Parker, Braunton
Port of Registry:	Bideford
Net Reg Tons:	59

First rigged as a topsail schooner. Was in the gravel trade to Bristol and grain and flour to N Devon ports. Condemned 1946. Her hulk lies on the bank of the River Torridge.

MAUDE MARY

Official number:	91320
Built:	G H Anderton, Howden 1889–1908
	William Quance, Appledore 1908–1918
	M Butcher, Yarmouth 1918–1923
	William Gibbs, Cardiff 1923–1925
	J Lamey, Appledore
Signal Letters:	L.B.S.V.
Port of Registry:	Bideford
Dimensions:	77.2 x 20.6 x 9.4
Net Reg Tons:	79

Converted to schooner 1930. Lost English Channel 1939. 50 h.p. engine fitted 1923. Finally sold to Michael Leszczyski of Poland.

MAY QUEEN

Official number:	62148
Built:	1868 Plymouth
Owners:	H Finimore, Plymouth
	H Stapleton, Bude
Signal Letters:	J.F.S.D.
Port of Registry:	Plymouth
Net Reg Tons:	49

MEIRION LASS

Official number:	24165
Built:	1853 Aberdovey
Rebuilt:	1877
Owners:	E Davies, Aberdovey
	W H Anstey, Cardiff
Signal Letters:	N.V.P.W.
Port of Registry:	Bideford

MERIDAN

Official number:	20663
Built:	1858 Aberystwyth
Builder:	J Evans
Owners:	R Francis, Aberystwyth
	E Hamblin, Bridgwater
Signal Letters:	N.C.D.M.
Port of Registry:	Bridgwater
Dimensions:	83.0 x 20.0 x 10.1
Net Reg Tons:	75

Grounded in fog 1921 refloated and drifted 100 miles to Camshore Point where she stranded and became a total loss.

MERLIN

Official number:	15330
Built:	1839 Bideford
Owner:	J Jones, Cardiff
Signal Letters:	L.R.T.W.
Port of Registry:	Barnstaple
Net Reg Tons:	16

MILLICENT

Official number:	19231
Owner:	H Tabb, Padstow
Signal Letters:	M.R.D.B.
Port of Registry:	Padstow
Net Reg Tons:	51

MILLBAY

Official number:	83941
Built:	1880 Stonehouse
Owner:	James Doyle, Kilkeel, Co Down
Signal Letters:	T.W.B.N.
Port of Registry:	Plymouth
Net Reg Tons:	49

Laid up at Upton on Severn 1944.

MINER

Official number:	10801
Built:	1830 St Helens
Owner:	S Ford, Saul
Port of Registry:	Bridgwater
Net Reg Tons:	43

A Severn trow.

MINERVA

Official number:	6378
Built:	1811 Newport, Pembroke
Owners:	R Allen, Watchet
	T Griffiths, Cheltenham
Signal Letters:	J.P.N.D.
Port of Registry:	Bridgwater

MINNIE FLOSSIE

Official number:	78475
Built:	1879 Hakin
Builder:	Davis
Owners:	P K Harris, Appledore
	Clayton, Appledore
Port of Registry:	Bideford
Net Reg Tons:	46
Dimensions:	60.0 x 18.0 x 8.0
Draught:	8.6

On degaussing service 1939–45. Lost off St Ives in storm
October 1945.

MISTLETOE

Official number:	93983
Built:	1890 Plymouth
Owner:	T Ley, Combe Martin
Port of Registry:	Barnstaple
Net Reg Tons:	45

Worked ports at western end of English Channel also carried
coal to the beach at Glenholme, Somerset.

MIZPAH

Official number:	108556
Built:	1898 Kingsbridge
Owners:	J N Phillips, Combeleigh, S Devon
	Allen, Watchet
Port of Registry:	Plymouth
Net Reg Tons:	38
Gross Tons:	120

Her anchor windlass preserved in the National Maritime
Museum. Whilst on passage Kilmore Quay for Cardiff with
potatoes struck sunken wreckage off Hook lighthouse
Wexford December 1928 and foundered.

Minnie Flossie

MONARCH

Official number:	105409
Built:	1890 Gloucester
Owners:	F A Healing, Tewksbury
	A S Rice, Gloucester
Port of Registry:	Gloucester
Net Reg Tons:	76

Lost off Eddystone 1917. (Another source says hulked at
Purton 1951). A Severn trow.

MORNING STAR

Official number:	70529
Built:	1878 Kingston, Elgin
Owners:	A Slogget, Padstow
	Corney, Braunton
Signal Letters:	R.M.G.V.
Port of Registry:	Padstow
Net Reg Tons:	100

MOUSE

Official number:	78426
Built:	1878 Drogheda
Owners:	Cardigan, Mercantile Co, Cardigan
	Harry Drake, Braunton
Port of Registry:	Cardigan
Net Reg Tons:	48

Lost in storm off Ilfracombe 1916.

MYSTERY

Official number: 78705
Built: 1879 Brimscombe
Owners: W Halling, Twining
G T Day, Tewkesbury
Port of Registry: Gloucester
Net Reg Tons: 41

A Severn trow.

NAUTILUS

Official number: 13499
Built: 1834 Hayle
Owner: W Facey, Ilfracombe
Port of Registry: Barnstaple
Net Reg Tons: 37

NAUTILUS

Official number: 14030
Built: 1835 Plymouth
Owner: J Bain, Lynmouth
Port of Registry: Barnstaple
Net Reg Tons: 61

NELLIE

Official number: 81983
Built: 1882 Littlehampton
Builder: J & W Harvey
Owner: Huxtable, Braunton
Signal Letters: W.L.V.G.
Port of Registry: Littlehampton
Net Reg Tons: 70
Dimensions: 85.3 x 19.1 x 6.8

Foundered on passage to Newfoundland.

NELLIE (or NELLY)

Official number: 63093
Built: 1872 Framilode
Owners: Thos Richardson, Chepstow
Wm Davis, Chepstow
Port of Registry: Gloucester
Net Reg Tons: 37

A Severn trow. Carried stone for Bristol, Newport and Avonmouth docks. Sank 1903 but raised and repaired.

NELLIE

Official number: 68200
Built: 1874 Barnstaple
Builder: William Westacott
Owner: F Drake, Wrafton
Port of Registry: Barnstaple
Net Reg Tons: 62

First rigged as a schooner.

Nellie Mary, Boscastle

NELLIE MARY

Official number: 83961
Built: 1882 Plymouth
Builder: R Hill & Son
Owner: W H Hutchings, Appledore
Port of Registry: Bideford
Net Reg Tons: 49
Dimensions: 64.0 x 18.6 x 8.1

NELSON

Official number: 3863
Built: 1804 Redbrook
Owner: P Clutterbuck, Whitminster
Port of Registry: Bristol
Net Reg Tons: 27

A Severn trow.

NEPTUNE

Official number: 43680
Built: 1863 Gloucester
Owners: F C Hipwood, Gloucester
C Nurse, Gloucester
Port of Registry: Gloucester
Net Reg Tons: 66

A Severn trow.

New Design at Lymsham Wharf, near Weston Super Mare

NEW DESIGN

Official number:	62979
Built:	1871 Bridgwater
Builder:	J Gough
Owners:	Colthunt Symons & Co, Bridgwater
	James Screech, Appledore
Port of Registry:	Bridgwater
Net Reg Tons:	50
Dimensions:	74.2 x 18.1 x 7.9

Originally rigged as a schooner. Was in the Hull and Aberdeen trade for some years. Laid up below Bristol bridge for some years up to 1946.

NEW LEADER

Official number:	68758
Built:	1873 Jersey
Builder:	Bisson
Owners:	T Jeune, Jersey
	Mead, Appledore
Signal Letters:	N.W.Q.V.
Port of Registry:	Ramsey
Net Reg Tons:	56
Dimensions:	72.8 x 18.2 x 8.8
Draught:	9.5

NORAH

Official number:	56365
Built:	1868 Bridgwater
Owners:	D Gower, Cardiff
	B Pearce, Highbridge
Port of Registry:	Bridgwater
Net Reg Tons:	59

A Severn trow. Became a hulk at Uphill in 1930's.

NOUVELLE MARIE

Official number:	69503
Built:	1869 France
Owners:	William Nolan, Shirken 1879-1888
	Island, Co Cork
	Mrs M Quance, Appledore 1888-1909
Port of Registry:	Bideford
Net Reg Tons:	40

Originally a two masted schooner, lost on Chapel Rock, Barry March 1909 when on passage Newport for Bude with coal.

NUGGET

Official number:	15563
Built:	1852 Charlottetown,
	Prince Edward Island
Builder:	William Heard
Owners:	W Blackmore, Fremington
	J Butler, Bickington, N Devon
Net Reg Tons:	64

First rigged as a polacca brigantine. Converted to ketch rig 1884. In trade until 1907 when taken to Bristol renamed *Mohawk* and used as a barge until 1924 when broken up.

OCEAN CHILD

Official number:	26714
Built:	1846 Runcorn
Owner:	C Camm, Framilode
Port of Registry:	Gloucester
Net Reg Tons:	46

A Severn trow.

OLIVE BRANCH

Official number:	76578
Built:	1878 Kingston on Spey
Builder:	Duncan
Owner:	A Ayre, Braunton
Signal Letters:	L.M.C.V.
Port of Registry:	Barnstaple
Net Reg Tons:	66
Dimensions:	78.3 x 19.5 x 9.4

Fitted with 25 b.h.p. Robey engine. Traded to Irish ports and in coal trade Lydney to Devon and Somerset ports. In 1925 lost mainmast and jiboom in heavy gale in Bristol Channel but managed to get into Ilfracombe for repairs.

OLIVE AND MARY

Official number:	77368
Built:	1877 Rye
Owner:	James Irwin, Combe Martin
Ports of Registry:	Gloucester
	Barnstaple
Net Reg Tons:	37

In trade until 1927.

OLIVER (subsequently renamed *Topsham*)
Official number: 77368
Built: 1871 Hempstead, Gloucester
Owner: Chas Silvey, Epney, Gloucester
Port of Registry: Gloucester
Net Reg Tons: 68

A Severn trow. At one time traded to Antwerp and Glasgow.
Hulked at Topsham.

ONWARD
Official number: 56368
Built: 1868 Sandfield, Gloucester
Builder: Evans & Knight
Owner: J Lamey, Appledore
    G Sulley, Bridgwater
Signal Letters: N.C.M.J.
Port of Registry: Bridgwater
Net Reg. Tons: 79
Dimensions:

On passage Newport for Court MacSherry with coal
December 1928 struck submerged object off Barrels light
vessel, Wexford and foundered.

ORESTES
Official number: 91802
Built: 1885 Plymouth
Builder: D Banks
Owner: T K Ridler, Minehead
Port of Registry: Bridgwater
Net Reg Tons: 49
Dimensions: 64.7 x 19.0 x 8.1
Draught: 8.9

Ran ashore on passage to Minehead with coal December 1926.
Nearly lost when failed to rise on tide. Later refloated. Was in
coal trade to Porlock until 1935 became a yacht and went to
Mombassa 1947. Sank in Tanga harbour in 1955.

OUSE
Official number: 26605
Built: 1884 Yarmouth
Owner: T Brooks, Appledore
Signal Letters: P.L.T.Q.
Port of Registry: Bideford

PALACE
Official number: 10887
Built: 1827 Brimstone, Gloucester
Builder: Wm Close
Owners: C Hobbs, Frampton on Severn
    H G Bryant., Bridgwater
Port of Registry: Bridgwater
Net Reg Tons: 43
Dimensions: 72.6 x 16.8 x5.1

A Severn trow. In trade until 1930's.

PARANA
Official number: 89
Built: 1852 Jersey
Owners: W Lewarn, Plymouth
    J Williams, Plymouth
    Vickery, Watchet
Signal Letters: H.B.K.V.
Port of Registry: Plymouth
Net Reg Tons: 60
Gross Tons: 100

PAUL PRY
Built: 1856 Iron Bridge
Owner: C Transon, Broxley
Port of Registry: Gloucester
Net Reg Tons: 22

A square sailed Severn trow.

PENQUIN
Official number: 19167
Built: 1858 Port Glasgow
Owners: Hammett, Lynmouth
    John Red, Porlock
    Edward Pedder, Porlock
Port of Registry: Beaumaris
Net Reg Tons: 51

Foundered 1901 in Bristol Channel off The Hangman. First
rigged as a smack.

PENRYN
Official number: 83853
Built: 1880 Falmouth
Builder: E Martin & Co
Owner: N S Furneaux, Penryn
Signal Letters: W.F.J.B.
Port of Registry: Falmouth
Net Reg tons: 61
Dimensions: 74.1 x 20.3 x 9.2
Draught: 10.0

Penryn

PILOT

Built:	1880 Bideford
Builder:	H M Restarick
Owner:	Stevens, Braunton
Net Reg Tons:	58

First rigged as a dandy.

PIRATE

Official number:	91454
Built:	1888 Stromness
Builder:	G & P Copeland
Owner:	R Drake, Braunton
	J Hartnoll, Braunton
Port of Registry:	Barnstaple
Net Reg Tons:	48
Dimensions:	57.2 x 19.3 x 8.0

Run down by a steamer from Cardiff.

PLEIADES

Official number:	74450
Built:	1877 Cowes
Owners:	Henry Drake, Braunton
	N Ayre, Braunton
Signal Letters:	K.S.T.W.
Port of Registry:	Barnstaple
Net Reg Tons:	45

In the coal trade to Barnstaple and gravel to Lydney.

POLLY

Official number:	42258
Built:	1858 Oldenburgh
Owner:	R G Sully, Bridgwater
Signal Letters:	T.K.H.O.
Port of Registry:	Bridgwater
Net Reg Tons:	163

POLLY

Official number:	62977
Built:	1862 Bridgwater
Owner:	C Boxley, Westbury on Severn
Port of Registry:	Bridgwater
Net Reg Tons:	22

A Severn trow.

POMONA (formerly *Bee/Richardson Queen*)

Built:	1846 Appledore
Builder:	John Goss
Net Reg Tons:	49

Built as a brigantine, later a schooner and then ketch rigged

PRIDE OF ANGLESEY

Official number:	27338
Built:	1859 Barnstaple
Builder:	W Westacott
Owner:	T Jones, Amlwch
Signal Letters:	P.Q.V.K.
Port of Registry:	Beaumaris
Net Reg Tons:	76

First rigged as a schooner.

PRIDE OF THE TAW

Official number:	62897
Built:	1870 Appledore
Builder:	A Cook
Owners:	R Wilkinson, Appledore
	Thomas Hare, Appledore
Port of Registry:	Bideford
Net Reg Tons:	50

First rigged as a schooner, later renamed *Pride of Mourne*.

PRIORY

Official number:	62799
Built:	1870 Milford
Owners:	Mrs Grace Incledon, Braunton
	F Drake, Braunton
Port of Registry:	Barnstaple
Net Reg Tons:	31

PROVIDENCE

Official number:	11694
Built:	1892 Tewkesbury
Owner:	J Bosley, Epney, Gloucester
Port of Registry:	Gloucester
Net Reg Tons:	45

A Severn trow. Smack rigged stump masted open trow with side cloths.

PRUDENCE

Official number:	11755
Built:	1822 Beathall, Salop
Owner:	William Cook, Saul, Gloucester
Signal Letters:	K.T.W.N.
Port of Registry:	Gloucester
Net Reg Tons:	59

A Severn trow in the coal trade Lydney to Bristol and Avonmouth.

PURSUIT

Official number:	44244
Built:	1862 Nevin
Owner:	Mrs L J Gill, Port Isaac, Cornwall
Signal Letters:	T.H.S.M.
Port of Registry:	Padstow
Net Reg Tons:	73
Dimensions:	73.5 x 20.6 x 10.2

Broken up 1929.

PURVEYOR

Official number:	13927
Built:	1810 Southampton
Owners:	W Maynard, Bude
	E Leonard, Bideford
Signal Letters:	L.B.K.M.
Port of Registry:	Southampton
Net Reg Tons:	33

Wrecked Bude sands 1898 whilst carrying bricks from Bridgwater to Bude. At one time went sealing in Antarctica.

Prudence at Bridgwater

PROGRESS

Official number:	86466
Built:	1884 Kingsbridge
Builder:	W Date
Owners:	Henry Grant, Kingsbridge
	Thomas Slade, Appledore 1912–46
	P Harris, Appledore 1950
Signal Letters:	J.N.T.S.
Ports of Registry:	Bideford
	Salcombe
Net Reg Tons:	76
Gross Tons:	85
Dimensions:	80.2 x 19.2 x 9.2

Sailed for 19 years in Newfoundland trade until 1908 crossing the Atlantic twice yearly. In collision on one voyage with an iceberg. Motor fitted 1919 when converted to wheel steering. Balloon barrage ship 1939–45. Hulk now lies at Angle Bay, Milford Haven.

Progress & Severn Trow Safety, Appledore 1950

Purveyor leaving Bude

QUEEN

Official number:	13173
Built:	1854 Gloucester
Owners:	Severn Canal Carrying Co
	D Gower, Cardiff
Port of Registry:	Gloucester
Net Reg Tons:	48

A Severn trow.

QUEEN OF THE WEST

Official number:	3877
Built:	1852 Honey Street
Owner:	I Rogers, Gloucester
Port of Registry:	Bristol
Net Reg Tons:	33

A Severn trow.

QUIVER

Official number:	26710
Built:	1852 Bideford
Builder:	Thomas Waters
Owners:	A Cook, Appledore
	C Lamprey, Braunton
Signal Letters:	P.C.G.Q.
Port of Registry:	Barnstaple
Net Reg Tons:	32

QUO ANIMO

Official number:	69905
Built:	1874 Saul
Owners:	H Nurse, Saul
	S Carter, Stonehouse
Signal Letters:	S.T.F.M.
Port of Registry:	Gloucester
Net Reg Tons:	89

A Severn trow.

R.T.B.

Official number:	79356
Built:	1884 Bideford
Builder:	Richard Blackmore
Owner:	A Hall, Bridgwater
Signal Letters:	J.R.M.B.
Port of Registry:	Bideford
Net Reg Tons:	45

RAINBOW

Official number:	28140
Built:	1860 Bideford
Builder:	Thomas Waters
Owners:	Silas F Jenkins, Appledore
	R Hooper, Appledore
	W Stevens, Braunton
Signal Letters:	P.V.F.W.
Port of Registry:	Bideford
Net Reg Tons:	57

First rigged as a smack. Lengthened 1869. Went ashore Lynmouth January 1923 on passage Ely to Bideford with coal and broke up.

RANGER

Official number:	9564
Built:	1797 Fishouse, I O W
Owners:	J H J Colsford, Cowes
	W Stokes, Weston Super Mare
Signal Letters:	K.H.T.N.
Port of Registry:	Cowes
Net Reg Tons:	24

Broken up 1909.

REINE DE PROVOYANCE

Official number:	55889
Built:	1867 St Irene
Builder:	C Raymond
Owners:	R Mac Morlano, Greenock
	James Sinnott, Clonackilty, Co Cork
	E Chugg, Braunton
Signal Letters:	K.C.P.Q.
Port of Registry:	Barnstaple
Net Reg Tons:	78
Dimensions:	85.0 x 22.7 x 10.2

Broken up Vellator in 1930's.

RELIANCE

Official number:	43667
Built:	1861 Cams Cross, Gloucester
Owner:	Stroud Gas Light & Coke Co,
Signal Letters:	T.P.W.C.
Port of Registry:	Gloucester
Net Reg Tons:	33

A Severn trow. Carried coal Newport to Stroud.

RINGDOVE

Official number:	19073
Built:	1863 Chepstow
Rebuilt:	1881
Owner:	T Cockle, Bristol
Port of Registry:	Bristol
Net Reg Tons:	49

A Severn trow.

RIPPLE

Official number:	105406
Built:	1895 Gloucester
Owner:	The Salt Union, London
Port of Registry:	Gloucester
Net Reg Tons:	30

A Severn trow. Hulked at Lydney 1954.

RITA

Official number:	51208
Built:	1865 Gloucester
Owners:	T G Beard, Gloucester
	Jenkins, Newquay
Port of Registry:	Gloucester
Net Reg Tons:	76

RIVAL

Official number:	93454
Built:	1887 Saul
Builder:	Evans
Owner:	D Sims, Saul
Port of Registry:	Gloucester
Net Reg Tons:	47

A Severn trow.

ROBIN HOOD

Official number:	3871
Built:	1852 Bristol
Owners:	G Sully, Bridgwater
	G Smith, Cardiff
Signal Letters:	H.W.D.B.
Port of Registry:	Bristol
Net Reg Tons:	39

A Severn trow.

ROSE

Official number:	85804
Built:	1882 Bristol
Owner:	A Johns, Gloucester
Signal Letters:	M.P.J.N.
Port of Registry:	Gloucester
Net Reg Tons:	64

ROSELYNE

Official number:	160352
Built:	1918 Gouda, Holland
Owner:	C T Dines
Signal Letters:	M.Q.C.Q.
Port of Registry:	London
Net Reg Tons:	87
Gross Tons:	138
Dimensions:	94.2 x 21.8 x 9.3

Built as a trawler. Sold to Denmark in 1949 renamed *Florrie* and subsequently *Uffe*. Believed afterwards sold to the West Indies.

ROSETTA

Official number:	97468
Built:	1890 Plymouth
Builder:	Watson & Fox
Owners:	S Chugg, Braunton
	Bennett, Appledore
Signal Letters:	Q.F.J.H.
Port of Registry:	Bideford
Net Reg Tons:	57
Dimensions:	76.3 x 19.5 x 8.7
Draught:	9.6

After the Great War was used for salvaging cargoes from sunken vessels in Kerry harbour. On degaussing service 1939-45. Lost off Barry 1945.

ROSIE

Official number:	79358
Built:	1885 Appledore
Builder:	Robert Cock
Owners:	George Hartnoll, Braunton
	G E Dedwith, Portmadoc
Signal Letters:	K.C.V.O.
Port of Registry:	Bideford
Net Reg Tons:	68
Dimensions:	83.0 x 21.0 x 9.9
Draught:	10.8

First rigged as a schooner. Motor installed 1920. In Newfoundland trade for many years. Finished her days as a hulk on the Pembrokeshire coast.

R PASSMORE

Official number:	96418
Built:	1890 Burton Stather
Builder:	T Garside
Owner:	D W Foreman, St Andrews, Fife
Signal Letters:	M.B.S.Q.
Port of Registry:	Dundee
Net Reg Tons:	79
Dimensions:	81.3 x 20.3 x 9.5
Draught:	10.2

Hulked at Uphill, Weston Super Mare. Sold for scrap £4 2s 6d, 1938.

SABRINA

Official number:	11349
Built:	1849 Tewkesbury
Owner:	W Hickery, Bristol
Port of Registry:	Gloucester
Net Reg Tons:	30

A Severn trow.

SABRINA

Official number:	99533
Built:	1893 Gloucester
Owner:	F Hipwood, Gloucester
Port of Registry:	Gloucester
Net Reg Tons:	89

A Severn trow. Broken up in 1930's.

Rosetta

SAFETY

Official number:	11118
Built:	1838 Stourport
Builder:	Thomas Drew
Owners:	F Jones, Newnham
	E Warren, Bridgwater
Port of Registry:	Gloucester
Net Reg Tons:	45
Dimensions:	63.4 x 13.0 x 3.5

An early Severn trow. Engines installed in 1931. Was trading up to 1949 carrying coal from Lydney to Bristol. Subsequently used for coal storage and was finally hulked on the banks of the Avon in Bristol in 1960's.

ST AUSTELL

Official number:	69841
Built:	1873 Portreath, Cornwall
Owners:	S Guard, Appledore
	G Clarke, Braunton
	Stribling, Braunton
Signal Letters:	W.S.L.G.
Port of Registry:	Fowey
Net Reg Tons:	57

First rigged as a schooner. Sank after fire off Wicklow about 1949.

SARAH

Official number:	43674
Built:	1862 Gloucester
Owners:	G Brocker, Framilode
	Weston Clevedon & Portishead
	Light Railway Co
	Mrs A Aldridge, Gloucester
Signal Letters:	T.P.W.L.
Port of Registry:	Gloucester
Net Reg Tons:	48

A flush deck Severn trow. Foundered off Lydney pier 1947.

SARAH ANN

Official number:	16940
Built:	1858 Newport, Mon
Owners:	J Tucker, Marwood
	Mrs E Tucker, Braunton
Signal Letters:	M.D.P.H.
Port of Registry:	Newport
Net Reg Tons:	45

A Severn trow.

SARAH ANN

Official number:	9484
Built:	1856 Padstow
Owners:	P Hawke, Liskeard
	P K Harris, Appledore
	R Tucker, Braunton
Port of Registry:	Fowey
Net Reg Tons:	75

SARAH JANE

Official number:	76348
Built:	1878 Salcombe
Builder:	Date
Owner:	T J Haynes, Sharpness
Signal Letters:	R.S.G.F.
Port of Registry:	Gloucester
Net Reg Tons:	47
Dimensions:	66.0 x 18.1 x 7.0

Wrecked off Ilfracombe.

SEAGULL

Built:	1858 Appledore
Builder:	William Clibbett
Owner:	Hockin and Hopper, Bude
Net Reg Tons:	54

Run down on voyage to Rotterdam in 1860's

SECRET

Official number:	60576
Built:	1867 Bridgwater
Builder:	J Gough
Owners:	T Harper, Saul
	H G Bryant, Bridgwater
Port of Registry:	Bridgwater
Net Reg Tons:	59
Dimensions:	75.2 x 18.3 x 7.1

SELINA JANE

Official number:	65312
Built:	1872 Bridgwater
Owners:	The Sharpness New Docks
	& Gloucester & Birmingham
	Navigation Co
Signal Letters	S.V.W.R.
Port of Registry:	Gloucester
Net Reg Tons:	68

SELINA MARY

Official number:	78081
Built:	1878 Calstock
Builder:	Edward Brooming
Owners:	C Hamley, Bere Ferrers
	George Irwin, Ilfracombe
Signal Letters:	R.H.L.T.
Port of Registry:	Plymouth
Net Reg Tons:	35
Dimensions:	59.0 x 20.2 x 7.1

First rigged as a smack. Mostly in the coal trade to N Devon ports. Went ashore Watermouth January 1916 but salvaged. Lost Ilfracombe 1916.

SEVERN

Official number:	21195
Built:	1858 Bristol
Owner:	Severn & Canal Carrying Co
Signal Letters:	N.F.H.W.
Port of Registry:	Bristol
Net Reg Tons:	65

A Severn trow.

SEVERN

Official number:	56363
Built:	1867 Bridgwater
Builder:	Watson & Co
Owner:	E & W Bagehot, Heale, Somerset
Port of Registry:	Bridgwater
Net Reg Tons:	75

A Severn trow. Converted into a barge at Bristol 1930. Hulked at Combwitch 1934.

SHAMROCK

Not Registered

Built:	1870 Falmouth
Builder:	Benjamin Blamey
Owner:	Benjamin Blamey
Net Reg Tons:	36
Dimensions:	52.6 x 16.6 x 6.5

A Severn trow.

SHAMROCK

Official number:	47054
Built:	1863 Hull
Owners:	R Gillan, Glasgow
	Mrs S E Lemon, Barnstaple
	W Williams, Braunton
Signal Letters:	V.B.M.T.
Port of Registry:	Middlesborough
Net Reg Tons:	77

Buried in seawall of River Taw after bank collapsed.

SHORTEST DAY

Official number:	58839
Built:	1870 Cowes
Owners:	W T Hart, Plymouth
	H Bird, Devonport
Port of Registry:	Plymouth
Net Reg Tons:	38

SIR FRANCIS DRAKE

Official number:	58361
Built:	1867 Barnstaple
Builder:	William Westacott
Owner:	F Drake, Braunton
Port of Registry:	Barnstaple
Net Reg Tons:	45

First rigged as a schooner.

SIR T D ACLAND

Official number:	29417
Built:	1861 Bude
Builder:	Stapleton
Owner:	G Irwin, Combe Martin
Port of Registry:	Bideford
Net Reg Tons:	35

Wrecked Bude 1887 whilst carrying coal from Newport to Bude.

SOUTHERN CROSS

Official number:	58365
Built:	1872 Barnstaple
Builder:	G W Westacott
Owner:	T Grimely, Dublin
Signal Letters:	K.W.T.J.
Port of Registry:	Jersey
Net Reg Tons:	54

First rigged as a sloop. Rerigged as a yawl and later as a ketch.

SPARTAN

Official number:	99539
Built:	1894 Gloucester
Owner:	A Johns, Gloucester
Port of Registry:	Gloucester
Net Reg Tons:	50

A Severn trow. Hulked at Broad Pill, Avonmouth.

SPEEDWELL

Official number:	11724
Built:	1840 Stourport
Builder:	J Jeffries
Owner:	H A Nurse, Gloucester
Signal Letters:	K.T.S.M.
Port of Registry:	Gloucester
Net Reg Tons:	61
Dimensions:	63.0 x 12.6 x 3.5

SPIRIT

Official number:	14678
Built:	1857 Cowes
Owner:	Robert Fisher, Appledore
Signal Letters:	L.P.D.M.
Port of Registry:	Cowes
Net Reg Tons:	44

Wrecked off Bude whilst carrying coal from Newport to Bude. Had previously lost all sails off Combe Martin in gale on passage to Lydney.

SPRIGHTLEY

Built:	1830 Padstow
Owner:	F Bunt, Tintagel
Port of Registry:	Padstow
Net Reg Tons:	38
Dimensions:	55.3 x 17.0 x 7.9

Lost on passage Swansea to Watchet 1909.

SPRY

Official number:	99538
Built:	1894 Chepstow
Builder:	W Hurd
Owner:	G Nurse, Temple Parish, Bristol
Port of Registry:	Gloucester
Net Reg Tons:	36
Dimensions:	71.0 x 9.0

Is probably the only surviving trow and the hull was recently taken to Ironbridge Museum, Shropshire for restoration. Traded until 1950. Traded below Worcester and in the Bristol Channel. A Severn trow. Was cut down to a towed dumb barge in 1920's.

SQUIRREL

Official number:	84671
Built:	1882 Bridgwater
Owner:	D Gower, Cardiff
Port of Registry:	Cardiff
Net Reg Tons:	56

STAR

Official number:	19049
Built:	1857 Scilly
Owner:	F Banfield, St Marys, Scilly
Port of Registry:	Scilly
Net Reg Tons:	68

Wrecked Porthminster beach St Ives 1900.

STAR

Official number:	10842
Built:	1820 Chepstow
Rebuilt:	1879
Owner:	E Hamblin, Bridgwater
Signal Letters:	K.Q.D.S.
Port of Registry:	Bridgwater
Net Reg Tons:	58

STRANGER

Official number:	29673
Built:	1862 Barnstaple
Builder:	John Goss
Owners:	William Dalling, Barnstaple
	Mitchell, Braunton
	G Manley, Braunton
Port of Registry:	Barnstaple
Net Reg Tons:	41

Originally sloop rigged. Later a smack and then ketch rigged. In the gravel trade to South Wales and coal trade to N Devon ports.

STRATHISLA

Official number:	27417
Built:	1860 Garmouth
Owners:	J Dimond, Chard
	C Petherick, Braunton
	G Chugg, Braunton
	Clarke & Stribling, Braunton
Signal Letters:	P.R.F.S.
Port of Registry:	Exeter
Net Reg Tons:	71

Stroud Packet at Bridgwater

SUCCESS

Official number:	29753
Built:	1861 Gloucester
Owners:	J H Westcroft, Droitwich
	The Salt Union, Liverpool
	G Sims, Gloucester
Port of Registry:	Gloucester
Net Reg Tons:	30

A Severn trow.

SUCCESS

Official number:	67654
Built:	1873 Bideford
Builder:	Thomas Waters
Owner:	F Lee, Bideford
Port of Registry:	Bideford
Net Reg Tons:	34

Built as a smack, later rerigged as a ketch.

Stucley, Bude harbour

STROUD PACKET

Official number:	11658
Built:	1823 Brimscombe, Gloucester
Builder:	D Ellis
Owner:	H G Bryant, Bridgwater
Port of Registry:	Gloucester
Net Reg Tons:	45
Dimensions:	64.5 x 15.3 x 4.0

A Severn trow.

STUCLEY

Official number:	22387
Built:	1839 Fowey
Owners:	Frank Hockin, Hartland Quay, N Devon
	W Bryant, Truro
Port of Registry:	Padstow
Net Reg tons:	32
Dimensions:	58.2 x 16.2 x 6.3

Traded to Hartland Quay. Became a scrap metal barge in Ireland at the beginning of World War II.

SUCCESS

Official number:	14788
Built:	1825 Bridgnorth
Owners:	J Smith, Saul
	G Sims, Gloucester
Port of Registry:	Gloucester
Net Reg Tons:	49

A Severn trow, stumped masted.

SULTAN

Official number:	48963
Built:	1864 Plymouth
Owners:	J Clarke, Braunton
	J & G Chugg, Braunton
Signal Letters:	W.B.C.G.
Port of Registry:	Barnstaple
Net Reg Tons:	49

Severely damaged in collision with *Amazon* Bristol, November 1922.

SUNBEAM

Official number:	99532
Built:	1893 Chepstow
Owner:	T Richardson, Chepstow
Port of Registry:	Bridgwater
Net Reg Tons:	54

A Severn trow. Still used as a floating workshop in 1950's at Worcester.

SUNRISE

Official number:	105408
Built:	1899 Bridgwater
Builder:	F J Carver
Owner:	O G Rudge, Bridgwater
Signal Letters:	S.W.N.G.
Port of Registry:	Bridgwater
Net Reg Tons:	79
Dimensions:	83.6 x 21.5 x 8.5

Sunk in S Edinburgh channel 1918.

SUNSHINE

Official number:	111391
Built:	1900 Falmouth
Builder:	Charles Burt
Owners:	Capt Lewis Nurse, Bridgwater
	Capt Screech, Appledore
Signal Letters:	R.T.J.K.
Port of Registry:	Bridgwater
Net Reg Tons:	76
Dimensions:	88.0 x 22.3 x8.8
Draught:	9.6

Went to Oran 1946 bound for Malta. Reported arrested by Italian customs for smuggling and last recorded Genoa 1951. Had a finely carved figurehead.

SUNSHINE

Official number:	89864
Built:	1890 Whitstable
Builder:	Whitstable Shipping Co
Owner:	H Williams
Signal Letters:	M.K.W.S.
Port of Registry:	Faversham
Net Reg Tons:	118
Gross Tons:	133
Dimensions:	95.8 x 23.3 x 9.0

SUPERB

Official number:	26782
Built:	1826 Bower Yard, Salop
Owner:	F Read, Bristol
Port of Registry:	Gloucester
Net Reg Tons:	51

SWIFT

Official number:	15540
Built:	1850 Pottington
Builder:	G Green
Owner:	F Lee, Bideford
Signal Letters:	L.S.Q.W.
Port of Registry:	Bridgwater
Net Reg Tons:	39

Smack rigged, then sloop and afterwards ketch rigged.

SUSANNAH

Official number:	63388
Built:	1871 Framilode
Owners:	H R Hyatt, Bristol
	G Dangerfield, Saul
Port of Registry:	Newport
Net Reg Tons:	61

SUSANNE

Official number:	28138
Built:	1860 Appledore
Builder:	William Clibbett
Owners:	Charles Brimacombe, Hartland Quay
	J M Cox, Appledore
	T K Pidler, Minehead
Port of Registry:	Bideford
Net Reg Tons:	36
Dimensions:	63.3 x 17.8 x 7.6

Lengthened 1875. Carried cargo to Hartland Quay until 1887 when pierhead washed away. Then Appledore owned. Rerigged from smack to ketch. In coal trade from Swansea, limestone from Caldy and slate from Delabole. Broken up Appledore 1924.

Swan leaving Bridgwater Quay 1911

SWAN
Built:	1884 Bridgwater
Port of Registry:	Bridgwater
Net Tons:	68

Sank after collision in Thames 1910.

THE
Official number:	125109
Built:	1908 Brixham
Owner:	T Harris, Brixham
Port of Registry:	Brixham
Net Reg Tons:	26

Hulk lies on the bank of the Torridge

TMP
Official number:	68862
Built:	1874 Portreath
Owners:	S Incledon, Braunton
	H S Clarke, Braunton
Signal Letters:	T.V.D.F.
Port of Registry:	Barnstaple
Net Reg Tons:	45

Lost when stranded on rocks near Ilfracombe 1917.

TAFF
Official number:	28504
Built:	1860 Bristol
Owner:	Severn & Canal Carrying Co, Gloucester
Port of Registry:	Bristol
Net Reg Tons:	67

A Severn trow.

TAVY
Official number:	95139
Built:	1889 Plymouth
Owners:	W H Ball, Plymouth
	South Western Brick Co, Plymouth
Port of Registry:	Plymouth
Net Reg tons:	25

TEAZER
Official number:	69452
Built:	1873 Barnstaple
Builder:	William Westacott
Owner:	J Hockaday, Delabole
Port of Registry:	Padstow
Net Reg Tons:	50
Dimensions:	64.0 x 19.3 x 8.3

First rigged as a smack. Lengthened 1896. Wrecked off Stepper Point 1901.

TELEGRAPH
Official number:	62971
Built:	1869 Barnstaple
Builder:	William Westacott
Owners:	W Webber, Minehead
	J Stoate, Watchet
	T Watts, Braunton
Ports of Registry:	Bridgwater
	Barnstaple
Net Reg Tons:	41
Dimensions:	61.0 x 19.1 x 7.7
Gross Tons:	70

First rigged as a smack, then a dandy and subsequently as a ketch. Foundered off St Anns Head when rudder case burst whilst on passage Newport to Wexford with coal in 1923.

THEODORE

Official number:	63091
Built:	1871 Saul
Owner:	D Gower, Cardifff
Port of Registry:	Gloucester
Net Reg Tons:	54

THISTLE

Official number:	91820
Built:	1887 Plymouth
Builder:	Watson & Fox
Owner:	J B Marly, Minehead
Port of Registry:	Faversham
Net Reg Tons:	53
Dimensions:	70.8 x 19.2 x 8.5
Gross Tons:	63

Lost Plymouth 1913.

THOMAS

Official number:	19279
Built:	1857 Bideford
Builder:	William Clibbert
Owners:	William Leonard, Bideford
	White, Braunton
Signal Letters:	M.R.H.F.
Port of Registry:	Barnstaple
Net Reg Tons:	40

First built as a schooner. Later rerigged as a ketch.

THOMAS EDWIN

Official number:	56658
Built:	Gunnislake, River Tamar
Builder:	Emmanuel Crocker
Owners:	Crocker & Martin, Calstock
	A Hiscock, Penarth
	P K Harris, Appledore
Port of Registry:	Plymouth
Net Reg Tons:	64

First built as a schooner. Lost in collision off Falmouth 1909. Was in trade to the St Lawrence in her early years.

THOMASIN AND MARY

Official number:	19226
Built:	1855 Boscastle
Builder:	T R Avery
Owners:	R D Blake
	R B Hellyer, Padstow 1855
	G Munro, Swansea 1856
	H G Hole & Llewellin Hole, Watchet 1858
	W J Lamey, Appledore 1919
	Scobling, Braunton
Signal Letters:	M.R.C.Q.
Ports of Registry:	Bridgwater
	Swansea
	Padstow
Net Reg Tons:	49
Gross Tons:	70
Dimensions:	55.8 x 18.1 x 8.2

Lost at Walton Bay, Portishead 1924 on passage to Hayle with barley.

THOR

Official number:	51202
Built:	1864 Gloucester
Owner:	F Hipwood, Gloucester
Port of Registry:	Gloucester
Net Reg Tons:	35

A Severn trow.

THORA

Official number:	98822
Built:	
Owner:	A Nicholls, Bristol
Port of Registry:	Bristol
Net Reg Tons:	78

THORNEY

Official number:	19235
Built:	1847 Langport
Owner:	J G Sully, Bridgwater
Signal Letters:	M.R.D.H.
Port of Registry:	Bridgwater
Net Reg Tons:	65

A Severn trow.

THREE SISTERS

Official number:	11095
Built:	1800 Plymouth
Owners:	T Ley, Porlock Weir
	E J Peddar, Lynmouth
Port of Registry:	Cowes
Signal Letters:	K.R.F.P.
Net Reg Tons:	42

Sunk English Channel 1921.

TILLEY

Official number:	63094
Built:	1872 Hempstead
Owners:	P Johns, Gloucester
	E T Hipwood, Gloucester
	W Everett, Bristol
Port of Registry:	Gloucester
Net Reg Tons:	70

TRALY

Official number:	128846
Built:	1912 Millwall
Builders:	Edwards & Co
Owners:	G Clarke, Braunton
	W H Petherick & Sons, Bude
Signal Letters:	M.D.V.G.
Port of Registry:	Barnstaple
Net Reg Tons:	70
Gross Tons:	108
Dimensions:	79.7 x 20.1 x 9.0

Traly leaving Avonmouth 1955

Built of steel with an 80 b.h.p. engine. Was in the brick trade to Liverpool. Sold to Norway and renamed *Karna* and was in general trade in the western Baltic. Subsequently renamed *Traly*. Owned by Christian Dueholm Partrederm in 1977 and in 1985 still working as a dredger from Remmerstrand, Norway.

TREBISKIN

Official number:	22199
Built:	1859 Padstow
Owners:	T M Gonvend, Wadebridge
	C M Evans, Portmadoc
	Chidgey, Padstow
Signal Letters:	N.K.L.V.
Port of Registry:	Padstow
Net Reg Tons:	59

Wrecked on Welsh coast.

TRIO

Official number:	298939
Built:	1862 Bideford
Builder:	Thomas Walters
Owners:	J Watts, Braunton
	H W Leslie, Appledore
Signal Letters:	Q.H.J.F.
Port of Registry:	Bideford
Net Reg Tons:	38

First rigged as a schooner. Later rerigged as a ketch.

TRIO

Official number:	72564
Built:	1876 Jersey
Builder:	Le Sueur
Owners:	De La Mare, Jersey 1877-1909
	W Slade, Appledore 1909-1919
	W Jones, Watchet
	Capt Warren, Bridgwater 1919
	W Escott, Watchet
Signal Letters:	T.N.W.G.
Port of Registry:	Bridgwater
Net Reg Tons:	77
Gross Tons:	81
Dimensions:	77.6 x 19.6 x 9.2

Engine installed 1926. Built as a schooner and rerigged as a ketch 1907. Was in the Newfoundland trade and later between Newport and Bridgwater with coal. Refitted 1935 and new keelson fitted. Went ashore Combwitch River Parrett 1939 and lost following capsizing.

TWEE GEZUSTERS

Official number:	85814
Built:	1876 Holland
Owner:	W K Clements, Bristol
Port of Registry:	Bristol
Net Reg Tons:	63

In November 1926 was in collision with Severn trow *Effort*. Had to jettison 50 sacks of wheat to avoid sinking.

Two Sisters

TWO BROTHERS

Official number:	56369
Built:	1869 Bridgwater
Builder:	J Gough
Owner:	J Herbert, Frampton on Severn
Port of Registry:	Bridgwater
Net Reg Tons:	52
Dimensions:	69.2 x 18.3 x 6.0

TWO SISTERS

Official number:	47889
Built:	1865 Bideford
Builder:	Thomas Waters
Owners:	P K Harris, Appledore
	J Chugg, Braunton
Port of Registry:	Bideford
Net Reg Tons:	62
Gross Tons:	79
Dimensions:	70.8 x 19.4 x 9.5

Originally built as a polacca schooner. Rerigged 1880 as a ketch was in the coal and brick trade in the Bristol Channel. Sank in 1922. Was raised and repaired. 40b.h.p. engine installed. Carried the last cargo of iron ore from Spreacombe mines near Braunton to S Wales. Bought for a voyage to Australia in 1939 but became a training ship for sea scouts at Littlehampton. Broken up in 1950. Said to have shipped the original rails for the Barnstaple to Ilfracombe line opened in 1874. Also traded to Ireland, Scilly Isles, English Channel and Bay of Biscay ports.

Trio of Bridgwater 1939. Moored off Black Rock river, Bridgwater

ULELIA

Official number:	74429
Built:	1877 Truro
Builder:	Charles Dyer
Owners:	John Estlick, Braunton
	William Drake, Braunton
	W K Slade & E Quance,
	Appledore 1899–1916
	Mrs Taylor & Percy Harris, Appledore
	Mrs Hobbs & John Hutchings, Appledore
Signal Letters:	R.B.K.M.
Port of Registry:	Barnstaple
Net Reg Tons:	58
Dimensions:	75.4 x 19.9 x 9.4

Was tiller steered. Built as a schooner. Rerigged as a ketch 1900. For many years in the Newfoundland trade and to Ireland. Lost by standing on rocks at Ross Carberry, Ireland, April 1930.

UNITY

Official number:	11649
Built:	1855 Gloucester
Owner:	Severn & Canal Carrying Co, Gloucester
Signal Letters:	K.T.M.N.
Port of Registry:	Gloucester
Net Reg Tons:	37

A Severn trow.

USK

Official number:	28507
Built:	1860 Bristol
Owner:	Severn & Canal Carrying Co,
Port of Registry:	Bristol Gloucester
Net Reg Tons:	39

A Severn trow.

VENUS

Official number:	93452
Built:	1887 Gloucester
Owners:	A Johns, Gloucester
	J Rice, Gloucester
Port of Registry:	Gloucester
Net Reg Tons:	57

VICTORIA

Official number:	19228
Built:	1847
Owners:	R Lobb, Port Isaac
	T Clarke, Wrafton
Port of Registry:	Padstow
Net Reg Tons:	40

Broken up at Vellator

VICTORY

Official number:	69918
Built:	1877 Gloucester
Owner:	J Herbert, Frampton on Severn
Port of Registry:	Gloucester
Net Reg Tons:	37

A Severn trow. Hulked at Chepstow.

VISION

Owner:	Clarke, Braunton
Net Tons:	80

Lost on passage from Appledore to Ireland.

VIXEN

Official number:	62677
Built:	1870 Newquay
Owners:	R Chichester, Braunton
	H Rouse, Lerryn, Cornwall
Signal Letters:	Q.N.M.B.
Port of Registry:	Padstow
Net Reg Tons:	35

Vixen and *Ceres,* Bude 1936 and *Mary Eliezer*

VOLUNTEER

Official number:	63092
Built:	1871 Gloucester
Owner:	The Salt Union Ltd, London
Port of Registry:	Gloucester
Net Reg Tons:	30

A Severn trow.

WASP

Official number:	119633
Built:	1895 Saul
Owner:	A S Rice, Gloucester
Port of Registry:	Gloucester
Net Reg Tons:	36

A Severn trow. Hulked at Lydney 1954.

WATER LILY

Official number:	78477
Built:	1879 Milford
Owners:	H J Solva, Pembroke
	Wm Warlow, Haverfordwest
	G & C Chugg, Braunton
Port of Registry:	Milford
Net Reg Tons:	24

WATER WITCH

Official number:	11656
Built:	1849 Stourport
Owner::	The Severn & Canal Carrying Co,
	Gloucester
Signal Letters:	K.T.N.B.
Port of Registry:	Gloucester
Net Reg Tons:	63

A Severn trow. Eventually became a motor barge.

WAVE

Official number:	29844
Built:	1864 Appledore
Builder:	William Clibbett
Owner:	J Day, Appledore
Signal Letters:	Q.H.J.N.
Port of Registry:	Bideford
Net Reg Tons:	55

Built as a polacca schooner then rigged as a brigantine a schooner and finally as a ketch. In trade until 1930's. Went ashore Saunton Sands November 1922. Refloated and repaired.

Wave at Lymsham Wharf, near Weston Super Mare

WESLEYANNA

Official number:	5528
Owners:	T Trick, Appledore
	G Butler, Braunton
Port of Registry:	Bideford
Net Reg Tons:	25

Wrecked Hartland Quay 1888.

W E GLADSTONE

Official number:	104023
Built:	1894 Galamton
Owner:	W H Podd, Lowestoft
Port of Registry:	Lowestoft
Net Reg Tons:	56

Wild Pigeon. Wrecked at Bude, February 1904

WILD PIGEON
Official number:	76251
Built:	1877 Dundalk
Owners:	J Connick, Dundalk
	Neal, Port Isaac
	N Tregaskes, Bude
Signal Letters:	Q.R.H.C.
Port of Registry:	Padstow
Net Reg Tons:	54

Wrecked when lockgates burst open Bude 1904. Swept out and became total loss.

WILFRED
Official number:	121606
Built:	1906 Milford Haven
Owner:	Mrs S Hancock, Milford Haven
Port of Registry:	Milford
Net Reg Tons:	31

WILLIAM
Official number:	13328
Built:	1846 Gloucester
Owner:	G F Peters, Bristol
Port of Registry:	Gloucester
Net Reg Tons:	63

A Severn trow.

WILLIAM
Official number:	3912
Built:	1809 Bower Yard, Salop
Owner:	E Hobbs, Highbridge, Somerset
Signal Letters:	H.W.G.R.
Port of Registry:	Gloucester
Net Reg Tons:	50
Dimensions:	65.0 x 15.0 x 3.7

Built as a square rigged trow. Later converted to ketch rig. Wrecked 1939.

WILLIAM
Official number:	26735
Built:	1837 Brockweir
Owner:	G Morgan, Saul
Port of Registry:	Bristol
Net Reg Tons:	72

A Severn trow.

WILLIAM
Official number:	11605
Built:	1841 Coalbrookdale
Owners:	B Pearce, Highbridge
	J Warren, Bridgwater
Port of Registry:	Bridgwater
Net Reg Tons:	52

A Severn trow.

WILLIAM
Official number:	11731
Built:	1826 Gloucester
Owner:	E Longney, Longney
Signal Letters:	K.T.V.B.
Port of Registry:	Gloucester
Net Reg Tons:	41

WILLIAM & SARAH
Official number:	19072
Built:	1860 Landogo, Mon
Owner:	W Williams, Landogo
Signal Letters:	M.Q.K.J.
Port of Registry:	Chepstow
Net Reg Tons:	44

WILLIAM & EMMA

Official number: 95138
Built: 1880 Stonehouse, Devon
Owner: H Gill, Penryn
J H Chubb, Penryn
Port of Registry: Falmouth
Net Reg Tons: 27

WILLIAM HENRY

Official number: 18367
Built: 1854 Feock
Owners: R Sampson, Devoran
Norman, Watchet
Signal Letters: M.L.N.J.
Port of Registry: Truro
Net Reg Tons: 70
Gross Tons: 87

WILLIAM MARTIN

Owners: F & E Corney, Braunton

Sunk by a U boat.

WILLIE

Official number: 99531
Built: 1893 Gloucester
Builder: Hipwood
Owner: Will Butler, St George, Bristol
Port of Registry: Gloucester
Net Reg Tons: 42

A Severn trow. Sank at mooring 1960.

WINIFRED

Official number: 108553
Built: 1897 Falmouth
Owner: Joseph Doney, Lostwithiel
Port of Registry: Plymouth
Net Reg Tons: 38

Traded ports of western end of English Channel. Supply ship to R N 1939–45.

WOLF

Official number: 45032
Built: 1862 Fowey
Owner: L Lawday, Appledore
Port of Registry: Bideford
Net Reg Tons: 76
Dimensions: 73.5 x 21.8 x 9.8
Draught: 10.7

Woodcock and *Lewisman* at Vellator 1939

WOODCOCK

Official number: 105768
Built: 1895 Plymouth
Builder: W S Kelly
Owners: D E Darby, Saundersfoot
T Bassett, Braunton
G Chugg, Braunton
Ports of Registry: Milford
Barnstaple
Net Reg Tons: 34
Gross Tons: 42
Dimensions: 61 Length
Depth in hold: 6.11

WYE

Official number: 19071
Built: 1860 Bristol
Owners: W A Osborn, Bristol
J Knight, Trellock, Mon
Signal Letters: M.Q.K.H.
Port of Registry: Chepstow
Net Reg Tons: 36

WYE

Official number: 28503
Built: 1860 Bristol
Owner: Severn Canal Carrying Co, Gloucester
Port of Registry: Bristol
Net Reg Tons: 57

A Severn trow.

Yarra

YEO

Official number:	29402
Built:	1862 Llanelly
Owners:	Thomas Lemon, Barnstaple
	J Light, Barnstaple
	T Butler, Braunton
	Packwood, Braunton
Port of Registry:	Bideford
Net Reg Tons:	43

Lost off Ilfracombe in heavy weather 1913.

YARRA

Official number:	83802
Built:	1880 Bristol
Owner:	D Gower, Cardiff
Port of Registry:	Cardiff
Net Reg Tons:	56

A Severn trow at first sloop rigged. Motorised 1949 and later became towed barge.

YOUNG FOX

Official number:	98396
Built:	1893 Goole
Owner:	C Symons, Bridgwater
Signal Letters:	N.F.C.R.
Port of Registry:	Bridgwater
Net Reg Tons:	78

ZENOBIA

Official number:	1700
Built:	1853 Barnstaple
Owner:	William Jackson, Yarmouth
Signal Letters:	H.L.C.J.
Port of Registry:	Yarmouth

First rigged as a schooner, later ketch rigged.

ZOUAVE

Official number:	18746
Built:	1858 Bideford
Owner:	J Finch, Clovelly
Port of Registry:	Bideford
Net Reg Tons:	68

First rigged as a schooner, later ketch rigged.

The following ships have not been traced:

BLAZER Built 1890.
FARMERS LASS Wrecked Bude 1902.
GEORGE CANNON
JANE EYRE Severn trow.
LANDS END
MARION LASS
MARIE EMILIE Severn trow. Stranded near Ilfracombe 1886 whilst on passage Newport to Barnstaple with coal, refloated and then broken up.
NELSON Owner – J Watts, Braunton.
NIGEL Severn trow. Registered – Bristol.
OCEAN GEM Owner – C Chugg, Braunton. Broken up Vellator.
OLIVE ANNIE Decked Severn trow. Still working until 1930's.
PRESIDENT GARFIELD Registered – Bideford. Lost 1906 off Bude.
WELLINGTON Owner – J Reverey. Registered – Bideford.
WILLIAM & MARTHA Owners–R & J Rowles, Clevedon.

Emma Louise, Appledore 1953

Maude, Barnstaple 1939

Dido C in drydock, Appledore

VESSELS BY PORT OF REGISTRY

ABERDEEN
Emma Louise

ABERYSTWYTH
Conservator
Lady Agnes

BARNSTAPLE
A T
Acacia
Ade
Alfred and Emma
Amazon
Auspicious
Bessie
Bessie Clark
Bessie Ellen
Bessie Gould
Bonita
Cambria
C F H
Cruiser
Democrat
Devon
Dido C
Dispatch
Edith
Emma Louise
Empire
Enid
F A M E
Fanny
Fanny
Fishguard Lass
Haldon
Heather Bell
Helstone
J M J
Jane
Jane & Sarah
John & Ann
Julie
Kitty Ann
Lenora
Linda
Maggie Annie
Marjorie
Mary Grace
Merlin
Mistletoe
Nautilus

Nautilus
Nellie
Olive Branch
Olive and Mary
Pirate
Pleiades
Priory
Quiver
Reine De Provoyance
Sir Francis Drake
Stranger
Sultan
Telegraph
T M P
Thomas
Traly
Ulelia
Woodcock

BARROW
Emily Barratt

BIDEFORD
Ada
Ade
Agnes
Alford
Alpha
Alwyn
Annie
Annie Davey
Ant
Argo
Bessie Wilkinson
Bonito
Brunswick
Caroline
Catherine
Charlotte
Coronation
Cornflower
D P T
Daring
Darling
Dewi Wyn
Dolphin
Eleanor Mary
Eliza and Ann
Elizabeth
Elizabeth Couch
Elizabeth Slown
Eliza Murray
Emblem

Emma
Emu
Endeavour
Florrie
Francis Beddoe
Friendship
Hawk
Heatherbell
Hematope
H F Bolt
Humility
Invicta
Iron King
Isabel
Jessamine
Jessie
Joseph or Thomas
Julie
Ketch
Kindly Light
Lady of the Lake
Leader
Lewisman
Lily
Lively
Lucy
Mabel
Margaret
Maude
Maude Mary
Meirion Lass
Minnie Flossie
Nellie Mary
Nouvelle Marie
Ouse
President Garfield
Pride of the Taw
Progress
R T B
Rainbow
Rosetta
Rosie
Sir T D Acland
Success
Susanne
Trio
Two Sisters
Wave
Wellington
Wesley Anna
Wolf
Yeo
Zouave

BEAUMARIS
Penguin
Pride of Anglesey

BRIDGWATER
Active
Ade
Adventure
Ann
Argo
Ark
Arthur
Aurora
Caerleon
Champion
Clara Felicia
Clareen
Crowpill
David
Duke of Wellington
Edith
Electric
Eliza
Elizabeth
Elizabeth Anne
Eliza Jane
Emma
Express
Fame
Fanny Jane
Florrie
Friends
Friendship
Gannet
Good Intent
Good Templar
Heatherbell
Henry
Howard
Industry
Irene
Jane
Julia
J Milton
John and William
Lavinia
Lizzie
Looe
Marian
Mary
Mary Louisa
Meridian
Miner

Minerva
New Design
Norah
Onward
Orestes
Palace
Polly
Secret
Severn
Sunbeam
Sunrise
Sunshine
Star
Swan
Swift
Telegraph
Thomasin and Mary
Thorney
Trio
Two Brothers
William
Young Fox

BRISTOL
Albatross
Ann
Ant
Alice
Atlas
Avon
Avon
Bertie
Black Rock
Derby
Duke of Wellington
Elizabeth
Eliza Jane
Emily
Emporer
Florence
Flower of the Severn
Happy Return
Independent
Ionadah
Lillea Venn
Mars
Mary
Mary
Mary Ann
Nelson
Nigel
Queen of the West
Ringdove

Robin Hood
Severn
Taff
Thora
Twee Gezuten
Usk
William
Wye

BRIXHAM
T.H.E.

BUDE
Joseph and Thomas

CAERNAVON
Clara Felicia
Conservator
Margaret Davis

CARDIFF
Caroline
Falcon
Kings Oak
Lark
Squirrel
Yarra

CARDIGAN
Annie
Eliza Ane
Mouse

CHESTER
Florette
J W V

CHEPSTOW
Industry
Joseph and Mary
William and Sarah
Wye

CHICHESTER
Humility

COWES
Crowpill
Daring
Martin Luther
Ranger
Spirit
Three Sisters

DARTMOUTH
Ceres
Louisa

DUNDALK
Lucie of Duldalk

DUNDEE
R Passmore

EXETER
Egremont
Haldon
Strathisla

FALMOUTH
Ailsie
Auspicious
Buttercup
Frances
Hobah
Penryn
William and Emma

FAVERSHAM
Sunshine
Thistle

FREETOWN S L
Gem

FOWEY
G H Bevan
St Austell
Sarah Ann

GLASGOW
Janette

GLOUCESTER
Ada
Alert
Alma
Anne
Arabella
Argo
Ark
Aurora
Beatrice Hanna
Bristol Packet
Brothers
Edgar
Effort

Eliza
Energy
Emily Priscilla
Epney Lass
Excelsior
Excelsior
Fame
Friends
Finis
Garibaldi
George
George
Georgina
Gertrude
Goodhope
Goodhope
Gloucester Packet
Hannah
Happy Go Lucky
Harriet
H H Wilton
Higre
Industry
Industry
Isabella
J & A R
Jane
Kate
Katie and Annie
Longney Lass
Lovely Susan
Lydney Packet
Margaret
Mary
Mary Ann
Mary Ann
Monarch
Mystery
Nellie
Neptune
Ocean Child
Olive and Mary
Oliver
Paul Pry
Providence
Prudence
Queen
Quo Animo
Reliance
Ripple
Rita
Rival
Rose
Sabrina

Sabrina
Safety
Sarah
Sarah Jane
Selina Jane
Spartan
Speedwell
Spry
Stroud Packet
Success
Success
Superb
Theodore
Thor
Tilley
Venus
Victory
Volunteer
Unity
Wasp
Waterwitch
William
William
William
Willie

GOOLE
Bernard
Buttercup
Charlotte
Daisy
Henrietta

GREENOCK
Mary Stewart

GUERNSEY
Cecilia
Johaan Carl

HULL
Amazon
Halcyon
Mary Eliezer

IRVINE
Lavinia

JERSEY
Annie
Bonita
Daisy
Emily
George May
Gorey Lass

Honour
Southern Cross

KIRKWELL
Haldon

LEITH
Lewisman

LITTLEHAMPTON
Nellie

LIVERPOOL
Ade
Brackley
Empire

LONDON
Crown of Denmark
Roselyne

LOWESTOFT
Gold Seeker
Greenwood Tree
W E Gladstone

MIDDLESBOROUGH
Shamrock

MILFORD
A T
Advance
Alice
Annie
Annie
Caerleon
Escort
Garlandstone
Howard
Kate
Lady of the Isles
Mary
Mars
Waterlily
Wilfred
Woodcock

NEWCASTLE
Amy

NEWPORT
Bristol Packet
Elisabeth
Emily Maria
Johnny Toole
Sarah Ann
Susannah

87

PADSTOW
Bluebell
Boconnoc
Ceres
Charlotte
Conservator
Cornish Lass
Emma Jane
Fishguard Lass
Frances
Jane
Jane and Sarah
Johann Carl
Lenora
Liberty
Louise
Millicent
Morning Star
Pursuit
Sprightly
Stucley
Teazer
Thomasin and Mary
Trebiskin
Victoria
Vixen
Wild Pigeon

PENZANCE
Duke of Cornwall

PLYMOUTH
Albert
Clara May
Diligant
Faith
Fanny
Flower O' Portsoy
Fishguard Lass
Hope
Little Jane
May Queen
Millbay
Mizpah
Parana
Selina Mary
Shortest Day
Tavy
Thomas Edwin
Winifred

POOLE
Ginevra
Hanna

PORTSMOUTH
Lady of the Lake
Mary Seymour

RAMSEY
New Leader

RAMSGATE
Elsie

SALCOMBE
Ann
Effort
Progress

SCILLY
Star

ST IVES
Cornish Lass

SOUTHAMPTON
Comet
Purveyor

SWANSEA
Jane and Elisabeth

Thomasin and Mary

TRURO
William Henry

WELLS
Herbert

WEXFORD
I'll Try

WOODBRIDGE
Bernard Barton

YARMOUTH
Zenobia

VESSELS OWNED AT APPLEDORE
AND BIDEFORD N DEVON

NAME	**OWNER OR MASTER**
Ada	A Goldsworthy
Alpha	J Cox
	W K Slade
Alwyn	J Mead
Argo	L Lewday
Aurora	J Butler
	J Cook
Bessie Wilkinson	P Wilkinson
Bonita	T Hutchings
Bristol Packet	J Slade
Brunswick	J Butler
Caroline	P K Haris
Catherine	J Hooper
	W Lamey
Charlotte	P K Harris
Cornflower	J M Cox
D P T	J Hooper
Daring	J Slade
Devon	J Butler
Dewi Wyn	Mrs L A Guard
Dispatch	J Cox
Dolphin	T S Owen
	W Jewell
Eliza and Ann	J Lemon
Eliza Murray	P K Harris
	Mrs Trick
Emblem	G Stoneman
Emma Louise	J H Gorvin
Empire	T H Fishwick
Fanny	W Slade
Frances Beddoe	Mrs B Beddoe
	P Harris
Gorey Lass	F Harris
Haldon	W Slade
Heather Bell	W Slade
Hematope	W Hutching
	G Eastman
H F Bolt	Capt Bolt
	W Fishwick
Hobah	C Lamey
Humility	T Pow
Invicta	J Jewel
Iron King	W M Acford
Isabel	W M Acford
J W V	W Slade
Jane	T Burnard
Joe Abraham	T Cook
Jane Ann Elizabeth	J Butler
Julia	B Lamey
Ketch	J Jewel
Lady of the Lake	Mrs S Quance

Name	Owner or Master
Leader	T Scilly
Lewisman	W Slade
Lively	W H Hobbs
Mabel	W J Land
Margaret	J Lamey
Margaret Davies	S F Ford
Maude Mary	W Quance
Minnie Flossie	P K Harris Clayton
Nellie Mary	W H Hutchings
New Design	J Screech
New Leader	J Mead
Nouvelle Marie	Mrs N Quance
Nugget	J Butler
Onward	J Lamey
Ouse	T Brooks
Pride of the Taw	T Hare
Progress	T Slade
Purveyor	E Leonard
Quiver	A Cook
Rainbow	R Hooper
Rosetta	Bennet
St Austell	S Guard
Spirit	R Fisher
Success	F Lee
Sunshine	Capt Screech
Susannah	J M Cox
Swift	F Lee
Thomas	W Leonard
Thomas Edwin	P K Harris
Thomasin and Mary	W J Lamey
Trio	W Slade
Trio	H W Leslie
Two Sisters	P K Harris
Ulelia	W K Slade
	E Quance
Wave	J Day
Wesleyanna	T Trick
Wolf	L Lawday

VESSELS OWNED OR SAILING FROM BRAUNTON NORTH DEVON

NAME	OWNER OR MASTER
A T	H Redmore
Acacia	W J Rogers, S Rogers
Ade	Ayre
Advance	Mrs A Incledon
Agnes	H Clarke
Alfred & Emma	H Clarke, Mitchell
Amazon	J Watts
	Mrs B Watts
Amy	J Crick
Ann	T A Slee
	C Chugg
Bessie	F Incledon, Clarke & A Chugg
Bessie Clarke	G H Clarke, G Gould Clarke
Bessie Ellen	J S Chichester, Mrs B Chichester
Bessie Gould	G Chugg
	G Clarke
Bonita	R Chichester
Cambria	J Chichester
	Mrs E Chichester
C F H	H G Clarke, Capt Striblng
Charlotte	Butler
Clara May	A Parkhouse
	Clarke
Comet	H Redmore
Crown of Denmark	W Hunt
Democrat	S G Clarke
	T & G Welch
Dido C	S Chugg
Dispatch	Paddison
Edith	H G Clarke
Elizabeth	W Drake
Elizabeth Anne	G Irwin
Elizabeth Couch	J Watts
Eliza Anne	G Clarke
Emma Louise	H & F Drake
	A Watts
Elsie	G Chugg
Emily Barrett	G Welch
Enid	W Chichester, R Chichester
Falcon	Clarke
F A M E	B Tucker, Stribling
Fanny	J Kemp
Fishguard Lass	G Chugg
Four Brothers	F & E Corney
Garlandstone	A & R Parkhouse
	J Newcome
Hanna	G Hartnoll
	A Watts
Harriet	T R Brown
Heatherbell	T Clarke
Helstone	J Watts
Honour	S Mitchell
	T Butler
Iron King	J Watts
Isabel	T Watts
	A Corney
Jane & Sarah	Mrs H Ayre
John & Ann	Chugg
	H Drake
J M J	C Hunt
Julie	J Chichester
Kate	J T Jones
Kitty Ann	G Chugg
Lady of the Isles	J Watts
Lark	J Chichester
	T Bassett
Lenora	Mrs M Chichester
Lewisman	Mitchell
	Capt Slatter

Liberty	J Watts
Linda	F Drake
Lucy	J T Moss
Lucie of Dundalk	Welch
Maggie Annie	A Corney, W Drake
Margaret	J Lamey
Marjorie	W Drake
Mary	Scobling
Mary Eliezer	G Clarke
Mary Grace	W Corney
	Clarke
	C Chugg
Mary Stewart	W Parkhouse
Maude	R Parker
	W Tucker
Merlin	
Morning Star	Corney
Mouse	H Drake
Nellie	Huxtable
Nellie	F Drake
Nelson	J Watts
Ocean Gem	C Chugg
Olive Branch	A Ayre
Pilot	Stevens
Pirate	R Drake
	J Hartnoll
Pleiades	H Drake
	N Ayre
Priory	Mrs G Incledon
	F Drake
Quiver	C Lamprey
Rainbow	W Stevens
Reine De Provoyance	E Chugg
Rosetta	S Chugg
Rosie	G Hartnoll
St Austell	G Clarke
	Stribling
Sarah Ann	Mrs E Tucker
Sarah Ann	R Tucker
Selina Mary	G Irwin
Shamrock	W Williams
Sir Francis Drake	F Drake
Stranger	Mitchell
	G Manley
Strath Isla	C Petherick,
	Stribling & Clarke
	G Chugg
Sultan	G Chugg
	J Clarke
T M P	H Clarke
	S Incledon
Telegraph	T Watts
Thomas	White
Thomasin and Mary	Scobling
Traly	G Clarke

Trio	J Watts
Two Sisters	J Chugg
Ulelia	J Estlick
	W Drake
Victoria	T Clarke
Vision	Clarke
Vixen	R Chichester
Waterlily	G & C Chugg
Wesleyanna	G Butler
William Martin	F & E Corney
Woodcock	T Bassett
	G Chugg
Yeo	T Butler
	Packwood

Appendix III

PRINCIPLE PLACES OF BUILDING AND NUMBER OF SHIPS BUILT

BIDEFORD	28
PLYMOUTH	22
GLOUCESTER	32
BRIDGWATER	22
APPLEDORE	18
BARNSTAPLE	17
JERSEY	12
BRISTOL	20
MILFORD	9
PADSTOW	10
FALMOUTH	8
CHEPSTOW	10
SAUL	10

Mary Stewart

Irene

Ann at Braunton Pill

Mary Stewart leaving Bude 1943

Rosetta

Mary Eliezer   Ilfracombe Harbour

93

WEST COUNTRY PORTS

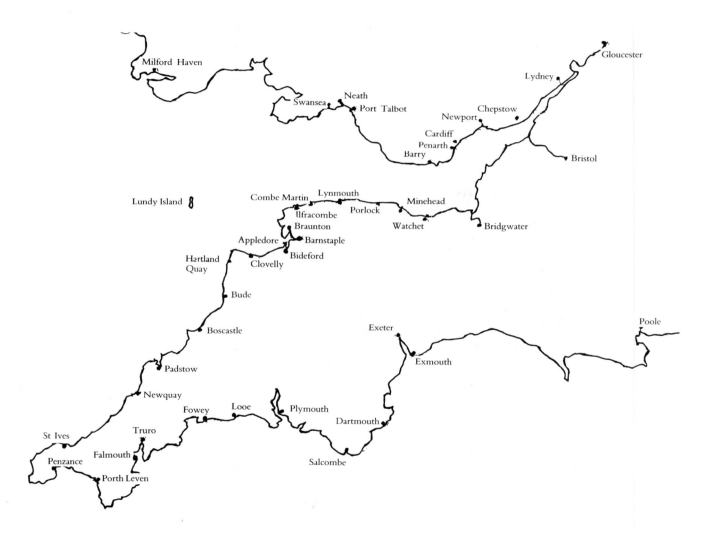

Milford Haven
Swansea
Neath
Port Talbot
Newport
Cardiff
Penarth
Barry
Chepstow
Lydney
Gloucester
Bristol

Lundy Island

Combe Martin
Lynmouth
Ilfracombe
Porlock
Minehead
Braunton
Watchet
Bridgwater
Appledore
Barnstaple
Bideford
Clovelly
Hartland
Quay
Bude
Boscastle

Exeter
Poole
Exmouth

Padstow
Newquay
Fowey
Looe
Plymouth
St Ives
Truro
Dartmouth
Falmouth
Penzance
Salcombe
Porth Leven

The Torridge Hulks

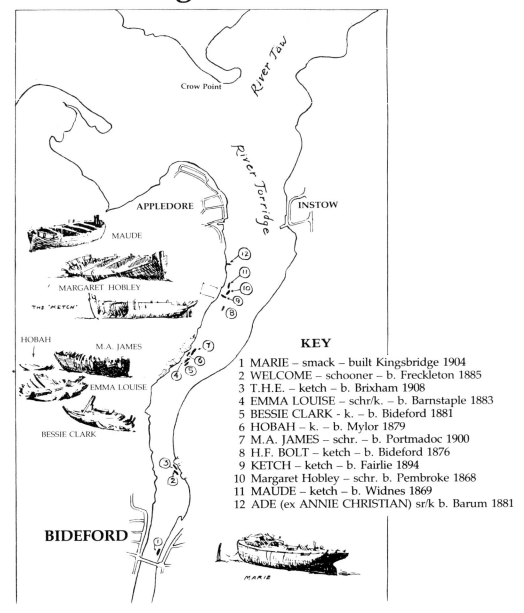

Crow Point

River Taw

River Torridge

APPLEDORE

INSTOW

MAUDE

MARGARET HOBLEY

THE 'KETCH'

HOBAH

M.A. JAMES

EMMA LOUISE

BESSIE CLARK

BIDEFORD

MARIE

KEY

1 MARIE – smack – built Kingsbridge 1904
2 WELCOME – schooner – b. Freckleton 1885
3 T.H.E. – ketch – b. Brixham 1908
4 EMMA LOUISE – schr/k. – b. Barnstaple 1883
5 BESSIE CLARK - k. – b. Bideford 1881
6 HOBAH – k. – b. Mylor 1879
7 M.A. JAMES – schr. – b. Portmadoc 1900
8 H.F. BOLT – ketch – b. Bideford 1876
9 KETCH – ketch – b. Fairlie 1894
10 Margaret Hobley – schr. b. Pembroke 1868
11 MAUDE – ketch – b. Widnes 1869
12 ADE (ex ANNIE CHRISTIAN) sr/k b. Barum 1881

BADGER BOOKS

The Heritage series looks at Devon as it is today and as it once was. The books attempt to preserve memories of bygone eras and also to record our County's history, both ancient and modern.

All the Heritage books are profusely illustrated with both new and many charming old photographs and prints, plus maps of the areas covered.

"Wildlife – Mammals" by Trevor Beer   £1.95

A clear, concise description accompanied by the author's illustrations of the principal mammals to be found in the Devon Countryside, from Red Deer to Pygmy Shrews.

"The Cruel Coast of North Devon" by Michael Nix   £1.95

Not merely a catalogue of shipwrecks, Michael Nix describes the agony of disaster and the efforts made to avert it from early lighthouses and lifesaving equipment down to the present day, ending with the wreck *Johanna* off Hartland point.

"Back Along the Lines – North Devon's Railways" by Victor Thompson   £1.95

Not written for railways enthusiasts alone, but a charmingly worded reconstruction of the history of the branch lines that did so much to improve communications throughout North Devon. Sadly, all save the line to Exeter have disappeared but fond memories linger on.

"Villages of North Devon"   £1.95
"Market Towns of North Devon" by Rosemary Anne Lauder   £1.95

Of interest to visitor and local inhabitant alike, the author has travelled throughout North Devon and describes in "Villages" those with something to offer in the way of history, or picturesque appearance, or true Devonian character. In "Market Towns" Barnstaple, Bideford, Hatherleigh, Holsworthy, Okehampton and Torrington are in turn studied with a history and a modern profile of each town.

"Lundy – Puffin Island" by Rosemary Anne Lauder

A discovery of Devon's mystical island, loved by all who know it, yet relatively unknown to many Devonians.

"Along the Shore" by Mike Towns

An exploration of North Devon's beautiful yet rugged coastline, its formation and its wildlife.

"A Herbal Folklore" by Anne-Marie Lafont

Fascinating remedies and old recipes from country kitchens in the days when the plants of hedgerow and garden were put to many and varied uses.

Also available:

"Vanished Houses of North Devon" by Rosemary Anne Lauder   £1.95

The story of six former mansions – Stevenstone, Eggesford, Dunsland, Annery, Yeo Vale and Winscott – now gone for ever.

"Tarka Country" by Trevor Beer   £1.95

Follows the story of Henry Williamson's famous otter "Tarka and his joyful water-life and death in the Country of the Two Rivers."

"Anthology for North Devon"   £1.95

A compilation of old and new – poetry, prose and photographs including the Devonshire dialect.